CITIZENS IN TRAINING

A MANUAL OF CHRISTIAN CITIZENSHIP

by

AMOS R. WELLS

AUTHOR OF "ELIJAH TONE, CITIZEN," ETC.

First Fruits Press
Wilmore, Kentucky
c2015

Citizens in training: a manual of Christian citizenship, by Amos R. Wells.

First Fruits Press, ©2015
Previously published: Boston, Chicago : United Society of Christian Endeavor ©1898.

ISBN: 9781621714170 (print), 9781621714187 (digital)

Digital version at http://place.asburyseminary.edu/christianendeavorbooks/7/

Wells, Amos R. (Amos Russel), 1862-1933.
    Citizens in training : a manual of Christian citizenship / by Amos R. Wells.
    105 pages ; 21 cm.
    Wilmore, Ky. : First Fruits Press, ©2015.
    Our workers' library
    Reprint. Previously published: Boston : United Society of Christian Endeavor ©1898.
    ISBN: 9781621714170 (pbk.)
1. Civics. I. Title.
BV1426 .W34 2015

Cover design by Jonathan Ramsay

asburyseminary.edu
800.2ASBURY
204 North Lexington Avenue
Wilmore, Kentucky 40390

First Fruits
THE ACADEMIC OPEN PRESS OF ASBURY SEMINARY

First Fruits Press
The Academic Open Press of Asbury Theological Seminary
204 N. Lexington Ave., Wilmore, KY 40390
859-858-2236
first.fruits@asburyseminary.edu
asbury.to/firstfruits

CITIZENS IN TRAINING.

A MANUAL OF CHRISTIAN CITIZENSHIP.

BY

AMOS R. WELLS,

AUTHOR OF "ELIJAH TONE, CITIZEN," ETC.

UNITED SOCIETY OF CHRISTIAN ENDEAVOR
BOSTON AND CHICAGO

C. J. Peters & Son, Typographers,
BOSTON.

Plimpton Press

H. M. PLIMPTON & CO., PRINTERS & BINDERS,
NORWOOD, MASS., U.S.A.

CONTENTS.

CITIZENS IN TRAINING.

CHAPTER I.

CHRISTIAN ENDEAVOR TRAINING CITIZENS.

THE millions of Christian Endeavorers in the world are in dead earnest — in *live* earnest, rather — on the great question of Christian citizenship. They are determined that saloon-keepers, the illiterate, the criminal, the corrupt and corrupting ward politician, shall no longer rule our fair cities or dominate our mighty nations. Scores of campaigns for the betterment of city life, through the reform of political abuses or the reform of individual men, have been carried on during the past few years by our ardent Endeavorers.

And yet only a beginning has been made. The government of America's cities is America's shame. If our great municipalities are to be redeemed within a generation from the foul hands into which they have fallen, the work must be done by the present Christian Endeavor host and their friends.

Who will pretend to say that conscience has anything to do with the politics of any of our great cities? Who will assert that the better elements are not cowed and held down and their influence reduced to *nil* by the lower elements? Were Alexander Hamilton alive, could he be elected mayor of New York; or Benjamin Franklin, of Boston; or William Penn, of Philadelphia? Are municipal affairs managed by the men most competent to manage them? The question, in its simple innocency, provokes a smile. As our cities have grown in greatness have their offices grown in honor? Has their political machinery improved and strengthened as more difficult work has been presented for it to do? In short, to sum up the entire arraignment, if an honest, clean, Christian young man were choosing a life-work, is not city politics positively the last occupation he would consider?

" O, you would bring Christian Endeavor into politics!" some one quavers. Yes, we would; into politics, but not into partisanship. Politics means, literally, the skilled management of a city, State, or nation. Outside of the Christian ministry, there is no occupation inherently more honorable and dignified and glorious than this of managing cities, States, and nations. In no way, not even in the pulpit, can the influence of a good and able man be exerted more powerfully than as mayor or alderman of a great city, legislator or governor of a commonwealth, or congressman or president of the nation. But we have driven our true leaders to become editors of daily papers, heads of reform societies, presidents of universities, or managers of vast, but private, business affairs.

It will be a sad day for Christian Endeavor when she mixes in party politics. May that day never

come. But the greatest bane of municipal government just now is that the national parties, formed
along the lines of national issues that have as much
to do with city issues as the eagle with the whale,
yet have assumed to themselves the rule of our cities.
Good citizens of all parties can combine in the interest of good city government without for a moment
losing their loyalty to their national parties, for those
parties have no vital or just connection whatever with
our cities.

There came one week from Philadelphia to Boston
a body of pilgrims. There were fifty of them, and
they were fittingly received in the Old South Meeting House, for they came to review the old landmarks
of that old town, to see just where the massacre took
place, and the tea went overboard, and the lanterns
flashed from the belfry, and the boys slid down hill.
As I listened to Mr. Mead and Dr. Hale and Colonel
Higginson and Lieutenant-Governor Wolcott and
Hezekiah Butterworth exploiting before that throng
of historical pilgrims from the Quaker City the glory
of Boston's past, I wondered if a pilgrimage would be
made, a century hence, from anywhere, to note the
memories of the great cities of to-day.

Towns are made great, not by vast buildings or
elevated roads or well-stuffed banks or marble pal-
aces, but by the great ideas that find expression in
municipal life. You young men that read this can,
if you will, add this decade a chapter to the history
of your city as glorious as Boston's revolutionary
decade. There yet remains many a revolution to

accomplish. Make your city — if you are in a metropolis — the first great city in the United States to adopt prohibition! You can do it. Throw all the rum into the nearest pond. That will be better than throwing the tea into Boston harbor, and will break the power of a worse tyrant than King George.

Make your city the first great city in the United States to establish the rights of minorities. Abolish the iniquitous and unjust ward system, whereby, if the lower element is in the majority in three-fourths of the wards of a city, it is impossible for that city to have a good government, even though the total vote of good citizens outbalance in the aggregate the total vote of the bad. Make it possible for the best citizens, from all over the city, to cast their vote for and elect a man worthy to represent them. Why should the votes of all the good men in my ward be rendered ineffective because there happen to be in the ward ten more bad men than good?

Make your city the first great city in the United States to break away, definitely and decidedly, from national party lines, and to divide its citizens into parties based solely, as they should be based, on municipal issues. In short, make your city stand for living issues, great ideas, and the manly embodiment of them. Thus you will catch up and carry on the Christian Endeavor watchword, " Christian citizenship!"

I call it a Christian Endeavor watchword, because Christian Endeavor is training the model citizen of the future. Better than that, Christian Endeavor is training the mothers of the model citizens that are to come. Let me point out four ways in which it is doing this.

In the first place, it is training young men and women in fidelity. No one can faithfully keep the Christian Endeavor pledge without becoming in political matters more faithful to his duty.

Citizens in Love with Duty.

That great word — *duty;* how I long to see it blazoned on the banners of all political parties, far above the tariff question, the silver question, and all other questions whatever! Citizens in love with duty, — that is what the nation needs; and to buy them she could afford to lose many cities. Citizens in love with duty, — that is what Christian Endeavor more and more is giving to the nation.

Christian Endeavor business men, whose ledgers will stand the audit of the recording angel. Christian Endeavor editors, whose leaders are not led by the advertising department. Christian Endeavor voters, who convert to truth that shallow pretext of the Orient, and make of their ballots veritable prayer papers.

Christian Endeavor policemen, that do not keep one eye fiercely on the front door of the saloon while the other winks at the side door. Christian Endeavor laborers, that would rather work overtime than undertime, and prefer to receive small wages rather than wages not fully earned. Christian Endeavor employers, who recognize a brother in their humblest servant, and hold themselves to be their brothers' keepers.

Christian Endeavor councilmen, that do not walk in the counsel of the ungodly. Christian Endeavor aldermen, that cannot be called paltermen. Christian Endeavor mayors, that do not with one hand hold majestically in front of them their staff of office, while the other hand is held out behind them for bribes.

Christian Endeavor legislators, whose bills are not influenced by a certain other kind of bills. Christian Endeavor governors, that do not confuse the rising sun on their State shield with the glimmer of the almighty dollar.

Citizens in love with duty, faithful citizens, courageous citizens, — these Christian Endeavor is giving to the nation, through its allegiance to its dutiful pledge, through its uncompromising and vigorous training in fidelity.

Citizens with Ideals.

In the second place, the Christian Endeavor movement is giving to our beloved nation citizens that are loyal to ideals. Our Society teaches love for ideals. No one has seen the church — that great church whose name we blazon on our banners — " For Christ and the Church"; yet to the eager eyes of these thousands of Endeavorers the Church is a splendid, visible reality. From loyalty to this unseen Church it is easy to pass to loyalty to an unseen political entity, a State.

The surveyor knows that the more ideal the point toward which he sights, the truer will be the line he draws. If he sights at a tree, his mistakes will be more mischievous than if he sights at a distant mountain top. If he sights a star, his aim will be truer still, and truest of all if he sights the unseen pole. Our Christian Endeavor pledge, while it turns steady gaze on things near at hand and definite, sights boldly along the line of high ideals.

It regards the local church, which we promise to support in every way. It regards also the universal church. It requires the specific daily prayer and Bible-reading, but also aims at the ideal, " whatever He would like to have me do," and " throughout my whole life."

So also the citizen that Christian Endeavor contributes to this nation will regard his practical, immediate, and definite duties to the state, such as voting, reading the newspaper, visiting the schools, investigating the characters of candidates; but he will also give zealous attention to building up the ideal commonwealth, making his State and nation the noblest possible instructor of the ignorant, supporter of the weak, director of the wandering, and rewarder of the strong. He will be a practical citizen, and for that very reason he will be all the more an ideal citizen.

He will not rest satisfied, in political any more than in religious matters, with the faithless cry, " Let well enough alone." Always before his eyes will swim the vision of the best. Always in his ears will ring

Christ's urgings toward the perfect. He will not let affairs take their course. He will not yield to sloth or cowardice or failure. He will have been taught in his Christian Endeavor training-school to pursue with vehement insistence the ideal, and to rest satisfied with nothing less.

Citizens that Pull Together.

In the third place, Christian Endeavor is bestowing upon this nation a blessing not commonly recognized; it is giving her a set of citizens that know how to co-operate, for common ends, with men of different views.

It has become notorious that, while parties appear to progress, the state seldom progresses with them. While the Democrats are hitched to the front of the car of state, the Republicans are hitched on behind, pulling in the opposite direction with equal strength. The next election may reverse the relative positions, the Republicans proudly stepping to the front and the Democrats sullenly hitching on the rear, but the wagon goes not a step farther for the change. Sometimes there are four parties, one attached to each corner, and then the car is almost torn to pieces among them.

Now Christian Endeavor would hitch the parties tandem. That is the Christian Endeavor way. In every deed there must be a leader. Christian Endeavor believes in leaders. But it also believes in co-operation, in pulling in the same direction.

In a Christian Endeavor union the president may be a Presbyterian, but all the other denominations hold up his hands. The largest society may be a Baptist one, but the other societies are not striving to draw away its members. When a Congregationalist proposes to the union a plan of work, the union does not reject it because a Congregationalist proposed it.

This co-operation does not mean that Baptists are coming to believe with the Congregationalists or either with the Presbyterians. They are not. But it does mean that all are believing most profoundly and zealously in Christ's one church, and eager to promote its interests first, their own interests second.

Such partisans in affairs of state Christian Endeavor is developing, — men able to see beyond the machine, the party, the platform, the offices, the majority of the moment, and willing to subordinate these at any time to the good of the state. Thoroughly believing in their own party and its principles, they are not so cynical or egotistical as to believe that all wisdom and patriotism lie within their party lines. They gladly recognize the good of their opponents, applaud their noble utterances, honor their worthy men, and even generously and patriotically assist them in their plans, whenever the people have placed their opponents in control.

It is the tandem principle. Under Christian Endeavor politics the state would move forward.

Skilled Citizens.

And fourthly, and finally, — though the theme is only entered upon, — one of the results of Christian Endeavor methods of work is the rearing of citizens trained to systematic and businesslike methods in the management of municipality and State — yes, and nation.

Much of current politics reminds me of a kind of band they have in Russia, as I have read. Each member of the band has a horn, which can give out only one note. If he is set to G, he can toot only when G comes in the course of the music. Most of his time he spends waiting for his turn to toot G.

Thus with our politics and politicians, — and we should all be politicians, taking the word in the old Greek sense of a citizen skilled in citizenship. A set of men is installed in the offices. They are police-men, postmasters, aldermen, mayors, legislators. It is their turn to toot G. " Turn the rascals out ! " is speedily the cry, and presto ! we have an entirely new set of officers, all tooting A. Thus, in swift succession, sound out the notes of our national anthem, whose words, being interpreted, virtually are, " Turn the rascals out, and let us toot."

Now Christian Endeavor does not play after the fashion of these Russian bands. It does not believe in this root-and-branch rotation in office. Its belief is expressed in the common Christian Endeavor for-mula : "A committee for every member, and every member on a committee." "All at it and always at it," full orchestra fashion, — that is what Christian Endeavor substitutes for the musical spasms of the Russian band.

Christian Endeavor believes in division of labor, but not in rotation of labor. There is in its work-shop a place for each, a task for each.

To go back to our musical simile, in its symphony of labor is a drum, — the social committee, that drums them up. There is a flute, a heaven-soaring flute, the prayer-meeting committee. There is a merry violin, the social committee, — a violin that sets hands rather than feet to wagging. There is the clarion call of the cornet, the missionary committee. All at it, and always at it, and at it all together, — thus goes the symphony of Christian Endeavor.

Now this spirit, applied to the making of a state, is giving to our country citizens constantly and defi-nitely at work for the public welfare. If on no other committee, they are on the committee of one, or the " whatsoever " committee. When they see a thing that needs doing, they do it, or see that it is done. They do not lazily and faithlessly delegate their citi-zenship to their rulers when they delegate to them authority to make laws.

Every Endeavorer has some little thing which he proudly does, regularly and carefully, for his society. It may be only to pass the singing-books or post the subject of the meeting on some bulletin board ; what-ever it is, his pledge holds him nobly faithful to it. Every Christian Endeavor citizen will also find his task for the nation of his love. It may be a slight

one, and he may not readily find it, but he will find
it, and will not be satisfied until he is expressing his
love for his country, and paying his debt to her, by
some sort of undelegated service.

The state cried : " Give me men, and the mothers
of men. Men who know their rights and dare maintain them. Men who know their duties, too, and
are swift to do them. Men of far-seeing eyes. Men
of generous, ready hands. Give me men, and the
mothers of men."

The merchant gave the state money, but that was
not men. The farmer gave her grain. The manu-
facturer gave her goods of iron and wool. The quarry-
man gave her stone. None of these were men.

The legislator gave her laws. The teacher gave
her formulas. The writer gave her paper, black and
white. Still the state cried : " I ask for bread, and
you give me stones. I need men — men, and the
mothers of men."

And to the state Christian Endeavor made answer :
" Here, my beautiful nation, here I bring you men,
and the mothers of men. Men of faith, and hope,
and love. Men of courage and steadfastness. Men
who honor their word, and honor God, and love their
fellows, and wish to serve the world. I give you
men," cried Christian Endeavor to the state, " men,
and the mothers of men."

CHAPTER II.

CHRISTIAN-CITIZENSHIP CLASSES.

IGNORANT EFFORT accomplishes little in any un-dertaking. Before our Endeavorers can do much along Christian-citizenship lines, they must study the problems of modern citizenship. This study, too, is the most appropriate work for young people, — far more fitting, in the majority of cases, than re-form campaigns or the purifying of political parties. In this chapter I wish to give an outline of a course of studies in Christian citizenship that may be made long or short, light or heavy, complete or fragmen-tary, according to the age, time, interest, and facili-ties of the society. If you enter upon it with zeal and wisdom, I am not afraid that you will not carry it on to a triumphant issue, not only in better in-formed citizens, but in some greatly needed concrete reforms.

First, as to the persons that will form the class. I strongly advise you, if your town or community is a small one, to join together in these Christian-citizenship studies all the Endeavorers of the place. You will gain the enthusiasm of numbers and the stimulus of one another's zeal, in addition to the great advantage of putting in a common stock the information each possesses already. Be strict in requiring attendance. Make it a privilege to join. Permit friends to be brought, but limit the number each member may bring. You do not want so large numbers as to quench the spirit of ready discussion. Moreover, the character of the work is degraded by the admission of many that do not " mean business."

Make it a point always to meet at the same time and place. Do not permit other interests to turn this aside. Advertise the class widely, and let entertainments avoid your evening, if they wish your patronage. Enter upon this work with the determination to place it first in your thoughts and plans, as its importance well deserves.

You will need a little organization. There must be a president to keep the meeting running on schedule time, and to preside over the discussions. There should be a secretary to keep the names and record of attendance, etc. A treasurer will be needed, to buy and sell the books you will study, if for no other purpose. You will find it advantageous to elect a librarian, to aid your members in hunting up books and articles on the subjects for investigation in the public library and elsewhere. You must have a programme committee, to obtain speakers and fix upon topics ; and you will need, for the most thorough work, an examination committee, who will prepare a set of questions on each branch of the study — questions that will not need many words for their answer, but yet will cover the ground fairly ; and this committee will read and grade the papers handed in.

The officers first named might well serve as programme and examination committees also, unless you have at your disposal a large union, and wish to interest many in the work.

Choose some text-book for systematic work, and get each member of the class to buy a copy, unless some prefer to own the book in partnership.

The best manual for your purpose will probably be " Christian Citizenship," by Carlos Martyn, D.D., sold by the United Society of Christian Endeavor for 75 cents. The programme committee will fix upon a certain number of pages to be read in preparation for each meeting. These are not to be read at the meeting, but at the homes, and part of the questions of the evening's examination are to be a test of this home study, the rest of the examination having to do with the class discussions proper.

Here is a suggested order of exercises for a meeting of the class : —

Opening devotional exercises.

Questions and discussion related to the section of the text-book for the evening.

Brief written examination upon the text-book and upon the points brought out by the speaker of the preceding week.

Address of the evening.

The speaker questioned by the members. A general discussion of the evening's topic.

Reports of special committees of investigation.

Announcement of the work next to be taken up.

Closing exercises.

The most important part of the preparation for a meeting is the obtaining of a speaker. It is not a good plan to allow one man to conduct all the conferences. No single man is at all likely to have the varied and vast stores of knowledge you will need. Seek out for each topic some practical man or woman — not necessarily a fine speaker — whose actual work has brought him the information you desire. Make everything bend to getting the right speaker. Do not hesitate to change the order in which the topics will be taken up, if by such a change you can obtain the best speakers. If you err in your choice, and are disappointed in the treatment of any subject, take it up again later on, with another man to treat it. Search a wide field for these speakers. Go into the next town, into neighboring counties, and into the near-by States, if your means or influence extend that far.

.And what topics shall you take up? I do not propose to lay down a scheme of study. Conditions are so different, — some that will use this manual being in the country districts and some in the large cities, and all facing their peculiar and individual local problems, — that to attempt to define one course for all would be absurd. My advice is that, in any case, you begin with the topic uppermost in public interest, whatever it may be. If you have been having trouble about your streets, study them ; if in the schools, investigate the public-school system. Branch out as your interest leads you. That is the secret of remembering what you study, and the secret also of winning popular interest to your class.

Let me illustrate by a list of subjects what you may study, with suggestions as to speakers : —

1. **The public-school system.** [Its history. The school board. The training of teachers. Teachers' examinations. How teachers are chosen. Teachers' pay. School discipline. The choice of text-books. School sanitation. The promotion of scholars. Truant laws.] This is a most interesting and important subject. It may well occupy several meetings, and be treated by several men ; for instance, some member of the board of county examiners, the school superintendent, one of the local school board.

2. **The streets and country roads.** [How a new road is laid out. How roads are kept in repair. How roads are paid for. The work of the street commissioner. Paving. Side-walks. The lighting of streets. Street franchises. The importance of better roads.] Here is another subject whose importance is fundamental, though it is not often understood to be so. Get some street commissioner to deal with it, and quiz him well. An old bicycle-rider will speak feelingly on the subject. So will a farmer.

3. **The temperance laws.** [Local ordinances. State laws. How saloons are licensed. The supervision of saloons. The number of saloons in the town. Probable expense caused by the saloon. New temperance legislation possible. Temperance education in the schools.] This topic should be treated by some well-informed temperance worker, preferably, of course, some lawyer. Make a map showing the location of all the saloons, churches, and school-houses.

4. **The building laws.** [Tenements and their condition. The crowding of population into the cities. Condemnation of buildings. Height of buildings. Inspection of buildings.] Obtain for this talk some architect or some building commissioner.

5. **The fire department.** [How it is manned. The engines and other equipment. The water supply available. Insurance rates. Selection and training of firemen. Improvement in this service.] By some fireman or some commissioner of this department.

6. **The police department.** [How policemen are chosen. What discipline they are under. Their temptations. The dangers they are exposed to. Changes needed in the force. The swearing in of deputies. Services policemen may be called upon to render. The board of police commissioners.] This talk may be given by a police officer, or by one of the commissioners.

7. **The public charities.** [The laws relating to paupers. The poor-house and the poor-farm. Pingree "potato farms." The causes of poverty.] The superintendent of the county poor-house may give this talk, or one of the county trustees.

8. **The prisons.** [The number of inmates. Routine of prison life. Punishments in prison. Liberties given the prisoners. Reformatories and their work. How the prison officials are appointed and paid. Changes desirable in the prisons. Work that Endeavorers might do there.] Some prison authority might be invited to give this talk, — the warden or the chaplain.

9. **The courts**. [The different kinds. Appeals from one to another. Judges, and how they are chosen. The duties of the clerk of court, of the sheriff, and other court officers. Who can practise at the bar. Legal abuses that need correcting. The jury system. The probate court. How to make a will. The police court. How to procure arrests. The grand jury and its work.] Of course this theme has almost infinite ramifications, and much judgment will be needed in selecting only the most practically important topics. Get some wide-awake lawyer to give this talk, and extend it to cover several sessions.

10. **Elections**. [Different kinds. When held. Registration. Residence required. Naturalization. Preparation of ballots. Oversight of the polls. Counting of votes. The report of the judges. The Australian ballot and similar reforms. Contested elections. Defrauding of ballot boxes. Changes that should be made in the suffrage.] Some one that has often served as judge of elections would be likely to talk to you helpfully on this important topic.

11. **The organization of parties**. [The caucus. The primary. The " machine." The political convention. Parties *vs*. independent action. How to gain influence in a party. How nominees are made. How a platform is prepared. Campaign expenses, and how they are met. National parties in local politics.] Get a politician to treat this subject. Better, get several politicians, one from each party; thus you will gain an insight into different methods, and you will see the matter from different points of view.

12. **The State legislature.** [Electoral districts. Names of your own representatives. When elections are held. How laws are made. Petitions. How to influence legislation. The initiative and referendum. The officers of the legislature. The payment of legislators. Their character. The governor and his duties. How the legislature gets through its work.] It goes without saying that a legislator himself would be the best person, probably, for this talk; though doubtless if you can obtain a newspaper correspondent of long experience, he would be quite as helpful, and even more entertaining. Several evenings could be devoted to this theme.

13. **The city and county organizations.** [The city charter. The city council. The mayor and his work. Aldermen: how elected, how paid, what they do. How an ordinance is passed. The county organization. What activities belong to the county, in distinction from the city.] The mayor, or one of the councilmen or aldermen, or some county officer, would be the best speaker on this subject.

14. **Our post-offices.** [Different classes of offices. How the postmasters are appointed. Their pay. Checks upon them. The importance of their work. How the public may aid the postmaster. Some needed postal reforms. Use of the mails for improper purposes. Evils of the spoils system.] Speaker: the postmaster himself.

15. **A free press.** [How newspapers are supported. The advertising patronage, and the influence it exerts. The editors' policy, and how it is

determined. How news is gathered. How a sub-scriber may help the editor. How we may better the tone of the public press. The power of the press, and how to enlist it on the side of good. The Sunday newspaper. The sensational paper. Use of papers by churches.] An editor or a well-informed, experienced reporter will be the man for this talk.

16. **Railroads**. [The electric road; its rapid progress in favor. The trolley system. The use of the streets. Three-cent fares. The influence of the electric car on the observance of the Sabbath. Steam railways. The effect of the Interstate Commerce Commission. Should railways be owned by the people? Should municipalities own their street-car systems?] If you have time, divide this subject into two evenings' discussions, getting men interested in the two kinds of railroads to treat each his specialty.

17. **The water supply**. [Reservoirs. Chemical examination of the water. The water-tax, and how it is adjusted. Penalties for non-payment. The use of wells and cisterns. Street sprinkling.] In connection with this subject, you may well take up similar questions regarding the gas supply, and the use of electricity. Some water commissioner will prove a valuable speaker. .

18. **The Sabbath**. [Sunday laws. New Sunday laws that should be framed. Church attendance. The theatre and Sunday. What stores may remain open? The Sunday saloon. Why this question should interest the general citizen, and especially

the workman.] Speaker: any well-informed citizen who has this theme on his heart.

19. **Orphans' homes and the like**. [This talk will include a discussion of lunatic asylums, homes for the aged, asylums for idiots, schools for the training of the deaf and dumb, and all such institutions.] If you can get some official from one of these establishments to describe its workings, it may serve as a sample of them all.

20. **Records**. [Where the public records are kept. Who is responsible for them. What they include. Marriages. Deaths. Mortgages. Deeds. Corporations.] The nearest register of deeds would probably give you a valuable talk.

21. ‹**The social evil**. [How far it is tolerated in your town. Is it protected by law? The theatre, the gambling hell, the race track, and similar themes may be discussed on the same evening.] Attempt to find out just how matters stand in your community, both as to law and as to fact.

22. **The public health**. [The board of health and its work. Druggists and their licenses. Who may practise as a physician? Sewerage systems. Municipal bath-houses. The value of parks. Public playgrounds and their usefulness. The examination of milk and meat. The functions of the State board of health. Regular inspection of homes.] Some physician should give this talk, preferably one that is a member of the board of health.

23. **The public library**. [Growth of public libraries. How the library is supported. Its officers.

Who chooses its books.   Proper and improper use of the library.   How to bring about the circulation of a better class of books.]   Speaker: the librarian, or one of his assistants.

24. **Taxes.**   [Assessments.   Who makes them. How they are made.   Boards of equalization.   What is exempt from taxation.   How the rate of taxation is determined.   Penalties for non-payment.   How citizens defraud the government of taxes.   Municipal, township, county, State, and national taxes.]   Best speaker: the township or county treasurer, or possibly one of the local assessors.

Of course these twenty-four topics will prove suggestive of a large number of other lines along which your studies may branch out.   Set no time for the completion of your course.   Make thorough work as far as you go.   Determine really to know something about the poor-house before you go on to the city treasury.

Follow up each address in some way.   The best way is to appoint a committee to study into whatever special matters connected with the topic may have excited interest, as shown in the discussions.   For example, the talk of the public-school superintendent may have led the class to suspect that the best text-books, under existing methods, are not chosen for your public schools.   Appoint a committee to study into this question, and to report later to the class. If this report has meat in it, get it printed in the local papers, and carry it out, or get your elders to carry it out, to further results.

These reports of special committees, whenever possible, should be embodied in careful papers. They may sometimes take the place of the evening's address, and may furnish matter for quite exciting and stimulating debates. If you want a vivid and thought-inspiring picture of the workings of such committees of investigation, read Washington Gladden's " The Cosmopolis City Club," published by the Century Co., New York ($1.00). Such original work will do more than anything else to extend the influence of the class, and make membership in it a thing to be sought after.

This plan presupposes weekly meetings. If you cannot manage that, monthly meetings will be better than none at all. The examinations I suggest need not be held, though I strongly advise them ; and, in short, any feature of the plan may be omitted or modified to suit local conditions. It is my decided conviction, however, that you will succeed far better in the work if you keep the requirements somewhat strict than if, for the sake of drawing in large numbers, you drop from the scheme whatever calls for a little work.

CHAPTER III.

A WORD ABOUT PETITIONS.

A GENTLEMAN, quite well acquainted with the feelings and work of legislators, once expressed to me his strong opposition to the use of miscellaneously signed petitions in an attempt to influence legislation. " The law-makers," he asserted, " are disgusted with them and pay no attention to them. They are well aware how little they signify, that they usually stand merely for some officious busybody who has been boring his friends, and that the legislators may with perfect safety to themselves absolutely disregard such impertinent requests. One communication," continued this gentleman," signed by a few thoughtful men, men the legislator knows and has confidence in, will outweigh a bushel basketful of ordinary petitions."

Now that is quite a statement. If it is true, — and I fear it is largely true, — then both the people and their representatives have been wrong; the people, in not making their signatures to petitions respected, and the legislators, in being unwilling to learn the will of the people, which, by the very name they have assumed, they have agreed to represent.

The right to petition is solemnly recognized in our constitutions. Is it our duty to exercise this right,

or is it a folly and an impertinence? After intrusting
our affairs to the hands of our law-makers, is it expe-
dient that we henceforward keep hands off until they
come around again for our votes? If anything is to
be said to them, is it only a few "thoughtful men"
that have a right to say it? Then in all logic those
few "thoughtful men" should cast the ballot for all
the rest of us at election time.

For a distrust of petitions is a distrust of democracy and a desire for an oligarchy. If the common
people are to be given the choice of legislators, it is
folly to deny them the right to influence legislation.
Indeed, it is already true that the vast bulk of our
State-house business is based upon petitions. Our
State legislators go up to their capitols loaded with
them. The committee on petitions is always busy
with hearings. Most laws spring from petitions.
But these are in the lower sphere of dollars and cents.
They concern bridges to be built, or court-houses to
be erected, or bonds to be issued. It is when by petitions men seek to guide legislation in the highest
matters, in great courses of policy, and especially in
moral questions, that the petition suddenly becomes
a nuisance and an impertinence.

There is no doubt that full many a crank has
chosen to turn this wheel of our political machinery.
Certainly there have been myriads of silly and futile
petitions, narrow, ignorant, and bigoted, signed by
hundreds of foolish zealots, and signed also by hundreds of men simply to get rid of bores. And because
most petitions of this class have dealt with moral

questions, though in a way almost immoral, many a legislator has come to throw all but purely business petitions into this class.

But legislators should discriminate, and we should discriminate. Indeed, when the level-headed citizens begin to discriminate, the legislators will. Never sign your name to a trivial petition, nor one crudely and foolishly worded. Never sign a petition when you are certain your representative will vote rightly upon the matter, unless you wish to support him in his position, or influence the legislative body in general, or show your colors for the good of the community at large. Never permit the petition to imply distrust of the legislator or of his associates. Do not permit this important matter of petitioning to get into the hands of ignorant or fanatical men. Anticipate them yourself, if need be. Already the best of our law-makers admit often that their course of action has been changed or modified through hearing from their constituents. They are glad to know their sentiments, and hold it a sacred trust to regard them, so far as their own consciences and knowledge will allow. Due care in the matter of petitions will increase this respect of politicians for their constituencies, and make more frequent the communication between them. Some one has fitly called the petition our " post-office referendum," and until our nation has advanced as far as Switzerland toward a true democracy, we cannot do better than use this irregular mode of getting the will of the people accomplished.

I should be glad to see the Christian-citizenship

committee in every Christian Endeavor society become also a petition committee — a committee whose
duty it would be to keep posted on the great moral
questions of the day, to learn the proper forms of
petition, to propose to the society subjects for petition when the need arises, and, after the executive
committee has voted on the matter and the pastor
given hearty assent, to canvass the society and community for signatures.

I do not suggest, be it observed, that the society
as a whole vote upon the petition. Such mass petitions, the expressions of mass meetings, conventions,
and the like, are of little value in influencing legislation. They are useful in emergencies, when there
is no time for more deliberate action, and they are
useful in arousing public opinion ; but they are far
inferior to an actual list of names.

Let the committee be sure that the petition is
couched in proper terms ; otherwise it will not carry
much weight, but will appear unbusinesslike and
crude. The forms of petition are straightforward
and simple, such as : " To the United States Senate : The undersigned hereby petition your honorable
body to — "; or : " To the United States House of
Representatives : The undersigned, members of the
First Presbyterian Christian Endeavor Society of
New York City, respectfully petition your honorable
body to — "; or : " To the Massachusetts House of
Representatives : The undersigned, citizens of voting
age resident in the City of Newton, hereby petition
your honorable body that — ."

Place your petition on heavy foolscap paper. Get some one that can write a plain, bold hand, to prepare the introductory address. Have separate petitions for non-voters. Get the signers to state their callings after their names. Sometimes it will be an advantage to state after each name the political party to which the writer belongs.

On the back of the petition, where it will strike the eye before it is opened, write, " Petition from —— for —— ," and place below a summary, such as: " Signed by 349 different persons, of whom 226 are voters. Of these, 18 are cl rgymen, 26 teachers, 13 editors and newspaper workers, 21 lawyers, 102 merchants," etc.

In addition, it will always aid your petition if you can accompany it with a letter from the strongest and best-known man obtainable, especially if he is well known to the representative you are addressing. This letter should be brief, but should call attention to the leading names among the signers. Thus, together with the popular demonstration, we get the influence of the " thoughtful few " urged by the friend from whom I quoted at the opening of this chapter.

In closing these directions for the effective use of this powerful political engine, I have three important points to urge. One is, be prompt. It is when a measure is in the early stages of discussion that petitions are most likely to be heeded. Keep your eyes open to what is going on. Your petition will receive double respect if its promptness gives proof of your energy, and that you are up to date.

Then, in the second place, follow up your petitions.   Learn with what consideration they meet.
If they are rejected, or the cause they plead, discover
why, and who is responsible.   You may have been in
the wrong.   If so, write to your representative and
tell him so.   If you still think yourself in the right,
let your representative know that he has not repre-
sented you, and that you will remember the fact.
It would not need many such letters to inspire in
the minds of politicians a very different opinion of
petitions.

And finally, though you will not petition so fre-
quently as to render your efforts commonplace,
though you will choose carefully among the many
good causes that might fairly become themes of petition, yet do not allow the exercise of this right and
duty to be neglected.   Your petitions, however numerous, will not lose force until you lose force.
There is an educative value in petitions that makes
it well worth while to petition, even if only to keep
the people wide awake and well informed.   You are
afraid your friends will think you a nuisance? Fear
rather that they and you will become careless and
indifferent to your political duties.   A citizen that
objects to signing his name to a petition, even as
often as once a month, may do so because he is too
lazy to write, or because he does not wish to take the
necessary trouble to inform himself and make up his
mind concerning the point at issue.   In either case
he is a fair object for patriotic missionary work.

CHAPTER IV.

REFORM CAMPAIGNS.

Non-partisan. It hardly needs to be said, and yet, in such a book as this, it must not remain unsaid, that all this work for better citizenship will fail of its results if it is not strictly non-partisan. In the selection of men to carry it on, in its approval or disapproval of nominees and measures, in all its sympathies, professed and implied, a Christian-citizenship movement must be entirely outside of party lines and above them. If, by a set of questions or otherwise, you think it best, the pastors agreeing, to apply a test to the various candidates for office, make your questions or other tests absolutely impartial, and present them to all the candidates, afterward setting all the responses before the people without comment. Never permit the movement to be drawn into denunciation of any party. Denounce principles and measures, but show yourselves as ready to uphold the good in one party as in another. In such municipal campaigns as you will conduct if you enter into practical politics, national parties have no business to meddle. The absolute divorce of municipal affairs from the national parties is the only condition of permanent success in any municipal reform movement,

Citizens' Movements. It is proper for our Christian Endeavor unions, as unions, to join in any citizens' political movements that are not organized in opposition to political parties, but it would be manifestly improper and unwise for a union made up of representatives of all parties by a majority vote to throw the weight of its influence against any one party. When party feeling enters into the matter at all, — where, that is, it is not merely a struggle of right against wrong, but also a contest between political organizations, — though Endeavorers may and should enter the contest as individuals, the Christian Endeavor union and its Christian-citizenship committee should maintain absolute silence.

Where such action would not jeopardize the higher aims for which Christian Endeavor exists, however, the Christian Endeavor union may even inaugurate citizens' movements. The Endeavorers may draw to their councils the wisest citizens of the place. They may, with their help, formulate a call to the decent men of all parties. At the mass meeting that will result, they may be ready to present a platform, and a set of candidates to stand upon the platform. They may appoint a committee of management, and carry on the entire campaign.

This advice, of course, takes it for granted that the Christian Endeavor union contains in its membership many men of ability and leadership, men who would attract followers and win and hold for such a campaign the respect it deserves and will need in order to succeed. In many a small town, — especially in the small towns where, through the lethargy of citizens, affairs have got into the hands of a few ignorant and corrupt men, — such a movement as this is the only way to rid the place of the incubus, and the young people may undertake it with the consciousness that they are doing God service.

You cannot go far in such a campaign without obtaining respectable candidates for the place from which you wish to oust the corrupt holders ; and here you will meet a serious obstacle. The offices have been so degraded by the occupancy of unworthy men that many of the best men consider it a disgrace to be elected to them. Besides, the salaries are so low as to afford no adequate remuneration for a prosperous business man who will not add to official emoluments by private plunder. You will need to hunt long, I fear, before you can find the necessary men of high character and position, who have enough of the spirit of self-sacrifice to accept nomination at the loss not only of personal dignity but of worldly wealth.

It will be a great help in persuading the best men to accept nominations, if you go to them bearing a petition to them signed by a large number of the best citizens, and asking them to take the nominations and make the campaign. No man of public spirit and true patriotism would refuse such a call, if it were at all possible for him to accept it.

As to the conduct of citizens' campaigns, the manner must differ so widely in different communities and under different circumstances, that any directions I might give would prove of little value. Do not make the mistake of relying upon any single method of influencing voters. Use the mass meeting, and the press, and posters, and personal conversations, and use them all with system and heartiness. If you elect your men, do not stand aside and expect them to carry out reforms without your help, but uphold their hands in every way. If — as is very likely — you do not elect your men the first time, keep a bold spirit and maintain the battle till victory is finally gained.

The Help of the Press. Do not scorn that mighty factor in all modern enterprises, the newspaper. If you can win its aid in your Christian-citizenship work, it is already half accomplished. If you cannot win its aid, you must overthrow it before you can go far.

In the first place, cultivate the editors and reporters. Do not take it for granted that even the worst of the papers will be out of sympathy with an honest reform movement.

Many of these sheets pride themselves on their full news reports, and will be glad to hear from you and print what you say, even though they may seek to contradict you on their editorial pages. Think twice before you raise an issue, by name, against any newspaper. You thereby convert it into a permanent foe. Use it as if it were your friend until you are absolutely certain that it will not be one.

Give all newspapers an invitation to your meeting, and provide equal facilities for all. Obtain for your letters to the paper, even for your notices of expected meetings, the very best writers you can interest in the reform. Many a reform movement has failed because its leaders, though capable executive officers, did not know how to write, but thought they did. Writing that is to push any reform movement should show great tact, unfailing courtesy, no flippant smartness, much wit and sprightliness, sound sense, unshakable accuracy, and then — after all these — as much eloquence as is convenient. No higher calling is possible for a man than to use his pen for the accomplishment of some moral reform ; but high tasks require high ability, and this writing is too often left to bunglers. What is well written — in the sense just defined — will find ready reception at the printing-office, and a respectful reading from any constituency. What is poorly written — slovenly, tactlessly or bombastically — is likely rather to harm than help the cause it advocates.

After all is done, however, it may be necessary, in order to win a victory over corruption, to start a reform paper and carry it on as a permanent Christian work. Of course such an enterprise — though it may be and has been initiated by Endeavorers — is too large for them to manage by themselves. Practical men with an abundance of money must take that work in hand. In the support of such a sheet, however, or of the papers already existing that place themselves on the side of reform if it becomes necessary to draw the line, the Endeavorers may be of the greatest service. They may canvass for subscriptions and advertisements, aid in the systematic collection of news, and talk up the paper or papers among their friends.

Even when no reform campaign is on, Christian-citizenship committees, purely in the interests of their work, should take up the activities of press committees, in case such a committee does not exist. It is of the greatest importance that the newspapers be kept informed regarding the enterprises of the churches, and none can collect this news better than the Endeavorers. The editors will be glad to receive it, if it is presented in workmanlike shape ; and, incidental to the publication of ordinary news items, there will come many a good opportunity to say a word for Christ and his church.

From Door to Door. An undertaking of great magnitude and of far-reaching possibilities for good has been inaugurated by the Evangelical Alliance of New York City, whose head is Rev. Josiah Strong, D.D. They are publishing a series of neat little pamphlets, written, in every case, by experts of national fame, and each treating some important phase of Christian citizenship. Some of them are occupied with valuable digests of the laws of the State in which they are intended to be distributed, — such laws as have moral bearing.

It is the hope of the Evangelical Alliance to enlist the young people in the circulation of these pamphlets, and better work for a Christian Endeavor Christian-citizenship committee could hardly be devised. The town should be districted among the members, and on a certain day one kind of pamphlet should be left at each house, with a personal call, — though brief, — and a request that the pamphlet be read. After a time, another pamphlet may be distributed, and so on. Careful selection of pamphlets should be made with an eye to the most pressing reform problems, and in the calls attention should be directed to whatever point in the pamphlets is of especial and immediate pertinence.

Of course this system of visits could be utilized with fine effect whenever it is necessary to arouse a constituency to prompt action on any moral question — when it is necessary that some immediate protest or appeal should be sent to legislature or Congress. These Christian Endeavor visitors, mounted on bicycles, many of them, will be all ready to circulate petitions, and, being already in touch each with his own district, would have ready access to the minds of the voters, and know just where to get the largest number of signatures with the least waste of time.

Before Election. How far the Christian Endeavorers should take part, as Endeavorers, in political campaigns, is a difficult and delicate question to answer. It would seem, however, that the Christian-citizenship committee might be able to do some few things in connection with a campaign without arousing just criticism. One is the obtaining of information about the candidates.

There is a great deal of voting in the dark, simply because the voters do not know how to find out about the men whose names are placed before them. The Christian-citizenship committee, by dividing among

them the list of candidates, each learning about a few,
could easily gather a great deal of valuable information which the Christian Endeavor voters, and doubtless many an older voter as well, would be glad to
use. Of course they would ask first about the moral
character of each candidate, and then about his at-
titude toward moral reforms. They would want to
know whether he was a drinking man, and whether
his allies were among the saloon-keepers. They
would look up his record, if he had been in office before. They would take pains to obtain accurate and
perfectly just information, and would sometimes ap-
proach the candidates themselves with testing questions. They would not put their information into
print, of course, but would simply give it out in private conversations to those that were in real doubt,
and seeking information.

If the committee are discreet and are fair toward
all parties, there is no reason why they should not
arm themselves with information on all sorts of public questions that have come up for settlement, and
so aid many a young citizen. If, for instance, there
is a proposition for more frequent elections, if a new
constitutional amendment is before the people, if the
school law is likely to be changed in some important
particular, — if any such matter of great importance
is up for consideration, let the Christian-citizenship
committee be ready to refer young voters to argu-
ments, articles, and books. The committee will show
its wisdom in refusing, under all circumstances, to
give any advice as to how any one shall vote, but will

simply set facts before him, or, better, set him in the way of finding out the facts for himself, and then let him decide for himself what his vote shall be.

Election Returns. The Christian-citizenship committee may arrange, for the benefit of the members and their friends, to receive the election returns in some hall where all can meet together. This will be especially appropriate when any reform issue is at stake. A group of neighboring societies or an entire union may combine for this purpose. The evening might be utilized in many pleasant ways, with social features, patriotic music, and recitations, but especially with the discussion of important reform topics, and addresses on Christian citizenship. Interspersed among these exercises the returns will be announced, and will be posted on prominent bulletins.

CHAPTER V.

CHRISTIAN-CITIZENSHIP MEETINGS.

A Flag Meeting. For this meeting decorate the room as elaborately as you please with the national colors. One or two talks might be given on the history of the United States flag. Most interesting material for these talks may be found in Townsend's "U. S. "(Boston : The Lothrop Publishing Co. $1.50). To illustrate these accounts, get the girls to manufacture a series of flags like those from which our national ensign was evolved, and hang them up one by one as the talk proceeds. A large copy of Washington's escutcheon should also be made. Besides, the nation has other kinds of flags, — the garrison flag, the Union Jack, the pennant, the revenue flag, — and these also should be obtained or made, and described. It will be of interest to make, also, a flag like one of those used by the Confederate States in the Civil War — perhaps their battle flag. If you can get them, or make them, show a few of the flags that are most like ours, such as those of France, Cuba, Liberia, and Chili, and note their resemblances. Compare also a few of the flags that are most diverse from ours, such as those of Japan, China, Austria, Persia. Pictures of these may be drawn, of large size, and colored.

Another part of the evening's programme will be the recital of some of the many stirring events in which our flag has played a conspicuous part. Dozens of them will come to the mind of any student of history. Divide these stories up, one to an Endeavorer, and insist that they be *told*— not written out and read.

There are many poems upon the flag. Make a good selection from these. Drake's magnificent poem will come to mind at once, " The Star-Spangled Banner," " Barbara Frietchie," and many more, for almost every American poet has a flag poem. Among the best of these is Holmes's " The Flower of Liberty." Some of these have been set to music and may be sung by a well-trained chorus. Extracts from " The Man Without a Country " and many another patriotic tale would inspire the audience with thought of what the flag means to the nation.

At this point you might introduce a salute to the flag such as is described in the chapter, " The Rescue of the Fourth." Another attractive feature of the meeting might be the formal presentation of a flag to the public schools of the town, if they are without a flag. Every schoolhouse should keep the national banner flying above it while in session.

If you can get some old soldier to give a talk about the flag, his memories of the scenes in which it has been prominent, you will be certain to listen to a speech that will fill you with deeper love for your country.

A good topic for the close of the meeting is this twofold one ; " What Christianity has done for our

flag, and what the flag means for Christianity."
Some good speaker may take this for his theme, or,
perhaps better, it may become the subject of an
" open meeting," in which all the members will par-
ticipate.

It will be seen that a flag meeting is full of pictur-
esque possibilities, and crowded with opportunities
for arousing patriotic thoughts. The outline given
for the United States will serve as well, merely chan-
ging a few terms, for any of the many lands into which
Christian Endeavor has been carried.

A Biographical Meeting. Such a meeting is
based entirely on the life of some great American,
say Garfield, or Hamilton, or Samuel Adams, or
Franklin. If you select a man whose birthday anniversary falls within the week or on the day of the
meeting, all the better. Obtain all the portraits of
the man you can, and hang them in view of the audience. Pictures of the houses in which he lived, of
the personages of the times, of the scenes in which
he was engaged, should be added to the collection.
Obtain also his autograph — in facsimile, if you can
do no better. You may be fortunate enough to get
hold of some relics of the great man you are to study,
or at least something that has come down from the
time in which he lived. All such articles should be
placed on exhibition. Old newspapers and books are
as suggestive as anything you could obtain.

Print clearly and post before the society a list of
the chief deeds in the life you wish to present. This
will serve as a back-bone for the meeting.

Your leader will open the meeting with a scripture reading appropriate to the national hero whose character you intend to display, followed by a suitable hymn. Prayers for the nation and its many interests may follow. Then the leader may give a short sketch of the life in its mere outlines — not too much for easy grasping and holding.

Others will follow with anecdotes concerning the man, each rising and telling his story in his own words, not reading it. Interpose extracts from his writings, together with recitations of poems that concern him.

The evening may close with three papers, one of them a general summary of his life ; one a comparison of his life with those of others ; and one of them telling the lessons to be learned from it.

In carrying out such a plan as this, much will depend upon the choice of a hero. First take stock of the literature accessible, and all other sources of information and illustration, and choose the man or woman about whom you have the prospect of obtaining the most that is interesting and helpful. Here is a list of names that may prove useful. Any of these would furnish material for a rich evening : Sumner, Webster, Governor John Winthrop, Samuel Adams, Lafayette, Andrew Jackson, John Brown, General Armstrong, Custer, Horace Mann, Garfield, Curtis, Lowell, Garrison, Patrick Henry, Grant, Grady, Lee, Franklin, Roger Williams, John Marshall, Jefferson, Wendell Phillips. Of course the list could be extended indefinitely, and I have purposely omitted, as meetings devoted to them are described elsewhere, the great names of Washington and Lincoln.

Patriotic Sharp-Shooting. A meeting with this title will be easily and attractively advertised, and will interest both participants and hearers. Give your orders for the meeting very plainly, and get the assent of the members, so that there will be no mistake about it.

Each will agree to furnish three things: one fact, one quotation, one desire. The fact will concern the nation — some statement regarding its greatness, — its size, population, products, achievements; any evidence of national growth that can be packed into a sentence or two. Limit the members to two sentences each, under this head.

The quotation will be patriotic, and in verse or prose. If verse, it must not go beyond one stanza; if prose, it must not contain more than three sentences. The name of the author must be given at the beginning of each quotation, as it is read.

The " desire " is to be some wish for your country's future. This may concern any reform you wish to see accomplished, any improvement you wish to see made. It may be expressed in prayer, when sentence prayers are called for, or it may be voiced in other ways.

The meeting will be divided into four parts, not including the leader's introduction, which should be short. First, the facts. They will be given in swift succession, and should be such as the following : —

" The State of Texas is as large as the six New England States plus the four Middle States, plus Maryland, Virginia, West Virginia, plus New Jersey, Connecticut, and Rhode Island measured over again. The entire population of the world could stand, without crowding, in a single one of the vast counties of Texas."

" Lake Superior is nearly four times as large as Massachusetts. On the waters belonging to the United States live many thousands of sailors, who are peculiarly hard to reach with the gospel."

" Our nation has had nine different capitals: Philadelphia at several times, also Lancaster and York, Pennsylvania, Baltimore and Annapolis, Maryland, Princeton and Trenton, New Jersey, New York City, and Washington. On the site of the present capital was a settlement called Rome, built on a stream still called the Tiber, the ground being owned by a man named Pope, which may be thought a prophecy of the present strong Catholic influence at the national capital."

After a bombardment of such facts, — to illustrate which, by the way, a map will be helpful, — call for the quotations. These will be found very easily. Take them preferably from the men that have been prominent in public life. For instance, the following : —

" The earnest, patriotic speaker and writer, George William Curtis, once said: ' By public duty, I mean simply that constant and active practical participation in the details of politics, without which the conduct of public affairs falls into the control of selfish and ignorant, venal and crafty men.' "

" A. R. Spofford, for many years the Librarian of Congress, declares that ' frauds upon the ballot-box should be ranked among the worst of crimes against republican government.' "

" Henry Clay said: 'Government is a trust, and the officers of the government are trustees, and both the trust and the trustees are created for the benefit of the people.' "

"George Washington said: 'The very idea of the power and the right of the people to establish government presupposes the duty of every individual to obey the established government.' "

" Said Daniel Webster: ' Let us remember that it is only religion and morals and knowledge that can make men respectable and happy under any form of government.' "

Then may come the expressions of hope for the nation, together with prayers for its interests. These will be followed by the fourth part of the programme, which may be a set address on some patriotic subject, by the best speaker the society can command.

A Bird's-eye Meeting. In this meeting you will attempt to arouse patriotism by showing the immense resources of your country, and the great good it may do with them. You will need to divide the themes among the members, or you will land in confusion. Let one have the task of illustrating the nation's wealth, another its area, another its population, — the mere bulk of it, — another the various races that constitute it. To others assign such topics as its schools, its churches, its newspapers, its climates, agricultural products, manufactories, excellences of government, the noble men and women of its history, its charities and philanthropies. Only a word can be said on each of the scores of topics that may be introduced.

The committee can help greatly to make the meeting effective by suggesting and helping in the preparation of maps and diagrams. For example, to show the size of the United States draw a large map of the country, and then set off upon it in different colors various foreign nations of the same area as certain groups of States, until the whole is covered.

To show the population, cut a long strip of paper, placing it upon a roller. Mark off a few feet in inches. Talk about setting a thousand men on each inch. Unroll it slowly, telling to how many thousand men you are thus giving room. When it has been unrolled across the room, say for how many thousand *miles* you must keep on in order to give room for the whole population of the country.

To show the races, draw a large circle, and color segments of it to represent the different races, each segment having a size proportionate to the number of persons that race has in this country.

To exhibit our variety of climates, show in swift succession a pine-cone from Maine, an orange from Florida, a lemon from California, flour from Dakota wheat, and the like. The more you present of such illustrations, the better will your facts and figures be remembered, and the more eager attention will they receive.

But do not permit this, interesting and valuable though it is, to override the main purpose of the meeting, which is to show how our great national resources should be used for Christ. Here again you must divide up the subject, and here you will need to use your best speakers. You can find time to treat briefly only a few simple topics. For instance, some one may say a word about the immense immigration to this country, and what good we are doing by training for upright and intelligent citizenship so many rude and ignorant foreigners. The reform of criminals, the example of a noble government afforded the world, the help we give to the darkened nations by foreign missions, — such themes as these may be discussed most profitably. It will require pains and planning to make this meeting the success it should be; but then, nothing worth doing is done without planning and pains.

A Great-Moments Meeting. The history of any nation will be found to be full of striking events — events that should not only be known to all citizens, but whose teachings are so clear and important that they furnish the best kind of material for thought at a religious gathering.

You will need to explain quite fully the purpose of the meeting. Give examples of the great moments you think worthy to be discussed. For instance, the call for volunteers for our Civil War, the Declaration of Independence, the assassination of Lincoln, the first step in teaching the first deaf mute, the first demonstration of ether, the signing of the Emancipation Proclamation, the first telegraphic message, the first steamboat voyage, the first use of the telephone, the first message over the Atlantic cable, the discovery of gold in California, the opening of the Centennial Exposition.

If the committee think it best, they may themselves form such a list and distribute the topics among the members, asking each to draw some lesson from the topic assigned him. The interpretation of the event need not be given in the member's own words. He may find words of Scripture, or some beautiful poem, that will say for him what he would like to say. This plan will give you, if it is carried out with sprightliness, a very lively and helpful meeting.

Bible Patriots. A Bible study in patriotism will be sure to set your society to thinking, and indeed it is wonderful how many fresh and pertinent lessons for our modern times can be learned from the lives of these ancient heroes. " What lessons for our nation and for our citizens from the life of Abraham ? " will be one of the questions propounded, followed by a long and noble list of Hebrew patriots.

The committee may throw out the question to the society without mention of any names, leaving it for each member to choose his own hero. Or it may apportion the patriots among the members, giving each a slip of paper bearing only one name. Or it may present to each a long and complete list, and ask him to select the one he would most like to speak about. The last way would be the best in most instances.

Here is a suggestive list : Abraham, Moses, Joseph, Samuel, Gideon, David, Asa, Joshua, Hezekiah, Elijah, Elisha, Isaiah, Daniel, Ezekiel, Amos, Jeremiah, John the Baptist, Paul. Of course Christ himself will not be omitted from such a list of patriots.

A Great-Leaders Meeting. For this evening ask each member to bring an anecdote of some interesting fact about some of the world's great patriots, and in a few words to bring out from it some lesson for American citizens. If necessary in any case, the committee should be ready to give help not only by naming men worth looking up in this connection, but also by pointing to different events in their lives from which lessons may be learned. Such leaders of men as Luther, William of Orange, Knox, Savonarola, Franklin, Garibaldi, and General Gordon will furnish forth a most inspiring meeting.

A Duty Meeting. "Our duty toward our country" — this theme, if well developed, would fill out a glorious evening. Try the plan of handing to each member a slip of paper containing the merest suggestion of the line of thought you wish him to take up at the meeting. For instance, the word, "Taxes," will suggest our duty to pay our just taxes promptly and without evasion; "Praise," will hint at our duty to say a good word for our country whenever we can; "Pray," will lead the recipient of the slip to speak of the duty of prayer for our rulers and our land. Other condensed hints are : "Write," "Money," "Study," "Fight," "Primary," "Vote," "Informed,"

" Brave," " Temperance," " Jury," " Homes," " Office," " Time." Some of these topics may be given to more than one. The committee will, of course, explain the meaning of the hint whenever it is not understood, and will stand ready to assist any one that wants help in getting something to say.

An Appreciation Meeting. " Why are you proud of your country ? " Ask each member to answer that question in his own way, and you will have an excellent and stimulating meeting. Throw out the hint that each should seek to give not the most obvious reason but one obtained by looking a little beneath the surface. It will be well, too, to ask the leading workers to come with several points, so that they need not repeat those given by others. Permit the members to illustrate their points in any way they please, and suggest that sometimes pictures, sometimes poems, sometimes songs may be introduced, and add emphasis to the points the members wish to make. Additional value will be given to the meeting, if the leader appoint some one to take notes and at the close to sum up rapidly the many reasons that have been given why we should be proud of our country.

Patriotic Quotations. A Christian-citizenship meeting easy to prepare, and very effective indeed, may be got up by simply giving to each member of the society some quotation bearing on Christian citizenship, and asking him to read it at the meeting, being sure to add some comment of his own. Ask him to tell who wrote his quotation, and suggest that very likely some good illustration of the quotation may be found in the life of its author. Many very fine extracts on a wide range of patriotic topics may be found in "Patriotic Citizenship," by General Morgan, published by the American Book Company, New York, and sold for $1.00.

A Gratitude Meeting. Especially near Thanksgiving time it would be appropriate to hold a "gratitude meeting," in the interests of Christian citizenship. The topic might be worded thus: "What our nation has done for the church, and what the church should do for the nation." See how many stirring themes may be treated under this head: —

Personal safety under our government.
 1. How it aids the church in its work. (Compare with other countries.)
 2. How the church can increase this safety.

Our public-school system.
 1. What it does for the church.
 2. What the church should do for the school.

Our national business prosperity.
 1. How the church is helped by the nation's wealth.
 2. What the church can do to increase the nation's riches.

The example of our great statesmen and warriors.
 1. How we may utilize it in our church work.
 2. What the church may do to better the quality of the average office-holder.

The nation's newspapers.
 1. What they do for the church.
 2. What the church may do for them.

A temperate nation.

1. How we lead in temperance principles and practices.
2. How the church can push the nation still further to the front in this regard.

These twelve topics are indicative of the wide range of subjects that may be taken up in such a meeting. Divide them among the members, assigning one to several members, if you please, and giving out quotations which those may read that have nothing to say of their own. Call for many prayers for our country, prayers of gratitude as well as of petition. Throw your whole soul into the meeting, and it will prove one of the best you have held.

Patriot Groups. A series of very interesting meetings may be built up by considering at each meeting the lessons from the lives of some group of patriots, such as the great orators of the nation. These may be treated after the fashion described in the section on biographical meetings, except that only a little can be told about each person, on account of the limited time. Simply one or two characteristic anecdotes will be enough, with the teachings of each. It will be the business of the committee to make a list of the orators that are to be discussed, and apportion them among the members of the society, letting each choose the orator he prefers to study.

Other groups for other evenings are: our great generals, patriotic citizens, great sailors, patriotic merchants, our patriot poets, patriotic women. The

Christian-citizenship committee, in preparation for such meetings as these, would do well to collect for some time previous as many interesting and pointed anecdotes as possible about our national heroes and heroines, or make memoranda of the books in which they are to be found, that the members may be guided in their search.

A President's Meeting. Of course many a patriotic and useful lesson may be learned from the noble men that have become chief magistrates of our nation, and an evening devoted to the studying of their lives would be well spent. Their portraits should hang about the room, as large in size as you can obtain. Add, also, pictures of their birthplaces, when you can get them, and of all other scenes connected with them. Assign one president to a member, giving the same name to more than one, if there are not enough to go around. Ask each member to come prepared to give some interesting anecdote regarding his man, and also to point out some lesson to be learned from his life. In addition, some of the Endeavorers may be appointed to read short extracts from the best of the writings of our presidents.

The presidents should be called for in chronological order, and before any member takes part, the leader should say a word about that president, aiming to present a very few of the facts regarding him that are most necessary to be known. For instance, name the one most important event of his administration; tell to what denomination each president belonged; name the political party to which each belonged ; give the date of his inauguration. The last is best shown by a large-type table posted before the society. Opposite this table, in the proper places, the leader may rapidly write a few words summarizing the facts he gives.

It will be easy to overdo this part of the programme. Remember that the meeting is not a history lesson, but is solely to get inspiration from these great lives. Close with prayers " for the President of the United States, and all others in authority."

This plan, of course, may be adapted easily to any other nation, and will furnish an especially rich evening in such countries as England and Scotland.

A View of Reforms. It will form a very good programme for some Christian-citizenship meeting if you make the evening a summary of the principal reform movements, trying to show their present status, with as much of their past history and purposes for the future as you can bring in. You will be able to get some specialists to speak upon their hobbies, (be sure to make them understand their limitation as to time !) but for the most part you will depend upon the Endeavorers themselves. You will want, of course, to treat the temperance question, although it must be treated briefly in such a meeting. You will add civil service reform, Sabbath observance, the divorce reform, ballot reforms, the initiative and the referendum, reforms in municipal government, progress made against speculation and gambling, suffrage reforms, the introduction of the curfew, the suppression of lynch law. Such a meeting as

this might wisely be followed by a meeting wholly
devoted to the lives of the great reformers, — lessons
from Garrison, Miss Willard, Bergh, Howard,
Gough, Comstock, Parkhurst, and other heroes and
heroines.

A Seal Meeting. A study of the State seals and
arms of our nation and of the various national seals
would fill out an evening of much interest and profit.
Many a helpful lesson could be learned from them.
Some are very suggestive; for instance, Utah's beehive,
Kentucky's clasped hands, Nevada's "All for
our country," West Virginia's "Montani semper liberi,"
— indeed, all of them have their points of appropriateness
and interest, and there are few, if any,
from which some good patriotic lesson may not easily
be drawn. The best way is to divide these State and
national emblems among the members, asking each
to discover the full significance of the one assigned
to him, and to come prepared to develop its meaning
before the society. In some way get large copies of
the seals made from the pictures in any large dictionary,
copies large enough to be seen readily across
the room. These should be exhibited one by one,
as each State is called, and then hung up so that at
the close of the meeting the walls are well covered.

CHAPTER VI.

TEMPERANCE MEETINGS.

OUR Christian Endeavor topic cards customarily contain each year four temperance topics. I wonder how many societies use them as genuine temperance topics, and how many take them in their most general aspect, shifting them, as far as possible, from the disagreeable and supposably worn-out theme of temperance! If this is the habit of some societies, it is because those societies do not know how interesting a temperance meeting may be made, and what a variety of fashions may be adopted in the conduct of them. Here are a few of them, and they may lead you to devise others.

A Bible Search. Divide the books of the Bible among the members of the society, asking each to bring to the meeting some account of what his book has to say on the subject of temperance. Thus the meeting will cover the entire Bible, and present a view which will be interesting from its completeness. Suggest that as many as possible commit to memory the passages bearing on the subject, and recite them. The leader should be prepared on all the Bible — you will need a good Bible scholar for a leader! — so that if any one is absent, his part of the work may be covered. Intersperse singing, and close with a five-minute talk by your pastor on the Bible and temperance.

A Biographical Meeting. The hour will be spent in a presentation of the interesting features in the life of some great temperance reformer. Such characters as Father Mathew, Miss Willard, John B. Gough, Lady Henry Somerset, Francis Murphy, John G. Woolley, Neal Dow, Mother Stewart, may be selected. It will be easy to obtain striking incidents from these strong lives. These should be *told*, and not read. You may take some single life, or a group of lives. For examples of the latter : " Some Noble Lives Spoiled by Intemperance " (such as Poe, Burns, Lamb) ; " Bible Heroes of Temperance "; " Women That Have Promoted Temperance." Hang portraits before the audience. Use extracts from the writings of those whose lives you treat. Have an appropriate poem or two recited.

An Historical Meeting. Much history has already been made by the temperance reform, and it is history well worth studying. What an inspiring hour, for instance, might be spent in telling the thrilling story of the Woman's Crusade ! Then, there are the Washingtonian movement, the " Blue Ribbon " movement, the World's Temperance Petition, the Maine law, and similar struggles in other States. " Temperance in the White House and the Capitol " would furnish an interesting theme. For this meeting get the help of some one who participated in the history you are to discuss, if you can find such a person ; and you probably can.

An Organization Meeting. An evening may well be spent in a bird's-eye view of all the temperance organizations, — the Woman's Christian Temperance Union, the " Y's," the National Temperance Society, the Good Templars, the national Prohibition party, the Loyal Legion, the temperance work of Christian Endeavor societies, the temperance societies among the Catholics, and the like. Facts should be presented about the form of organization of each, the way they are supported, their great leaders, their triumphs, their methods, their aims. Have, to give away, samples of the literature published by each, especially of the temperance periodicals. It would be a good plan to assign some one organization to each committee, and call upon each, in turn, to present its subject as it pleases.

A Newspaper Meeting. There is always a great deal in the newspapers that bears more or less directly on temperance. It will result in a valuable meeting if you set your Endeavorers to ferreting out these items. Some of the States may have just passed through a campaign with reference to prohibition. In some of the States, according to law, this question must be submitted to the people every year. In a neighboring city a stirring temperance address may have been made, and you can get reports of it. Some of the great temperance organizations have held their annual conventions. Some business man has fallen, his ruin being traceable to drink. A murder has been committed by a man under the influence of liquor. Disclosures of distress among the poor have been made ; and poverty, in nearly every case, is the result of strong drink. The elections of some great city are under the control of the rum power and evil men are getting into office. Such facts as these may be found in abundance. Explain the plan fully to the society, and offer to aid those that have difficulty in finding items, and you will have a good meeting — one that will be especially strong because of its freshness and undoubted authenticity.

A Map Meeting. Draw a map of the entire city showing the streets plainly enough to be seen across the room. Divide the city into districts, and send the members of the society to locate each saloon, church, and school-house. At the meeting, as these reports are given, some one will stand before the society and place "stickers" on the map, — black for each saloon, red for each school-house, and blue for each church. On the conclusion, let some good speaker draw the moral in a five-minute talk. On another occasion, or on the same evening, if you have time for it, draw a large outline map of the United States, and prepare also dissected maps of the different States. These will be colored to represent the kind and extent of temperance legislation so far adopted in each. For instance, all that have the Massachusetts plan will be of one color; the South Carolina plan, another; the Maine plan, another; the Ohio plan, another. Of course a careful explanation must be given of what each plan is. The States will be pinned upon a large map one by one, as the temperance status of each is set forth, and the result will be a large amount of temperance information very pleasantly imbibed and digested.

A Statistics Meeting. In this meeting try to make vivid the tremendous meaning of temperance statistics. The temperance committee will provide a large number of these, obtaining them from the National Temperance Almanac (published by the National Temperance Society, New York) and from similar sources. These figures are to be treated in different ways. Some — the more backward — may simply be asked to read them. Others may be trusted to illustrate their figures with their own devices. The most you will have to show what you want them to do. For instance, giving one the number of drunkards that die every year in this country, ask him to get a line of boys to march across the room before the audience, after which he will tell how long would be the column of drunkards that die every year, if they should march past at the same rate. Give to another member the number of saloons in the country and the number of church buildings. Ask him to figure out and tell the audience how long streets each would make. Tell another how much money is spent for strong drink each year, and ask him to imagine an equivalent pile of silver dollars, and find out how high a column they would make. With strips of paper of various lengths, with squares of different sizes and colors, with blocks of wood, and pictures, and all sorts of diagrams, you can make even the driest set of figures as interesting as a fairy tale.

A Quotations Meeting. Ask each Endeavorer to bring to the meeting some brief quotation bearing on temperance. Give the widest liberty. It may be in prose or poetry, figures or fancy, anecdote or exhortation. Urge each member to make some comment on what he reads. Strictly limit each to one minute or less. Intersperse singing. Close with a strong temperance address which will bring together some of the most striking thoughts that have been expressed.

Other Plans. A few methods may be mentioned more briefly. Devote the entire time at some meeting to a temperance address, if you can get some eloquent or practical speaker. Get some teacher of temperance in the public schools to give a talk on the physiological effects of alcohol, illustrated by some of the convincing experiments that are described in temperance physiologies. Try a debate on some topic connected with temperance. This debate should not be long, of course, but should be dignified, and appropriate to a meeting held on the Sabbath. Present an occasional number of a temperance paper edited — in manuscript, of course — by one of the society, but with contributions of all kinds from all the members. " The Cold Water Herald " would be a good name for it. Finally, and most important of all, hold some time a pledge meeting, in which will be urged, as powerfully as you can get it urged, the wisdom and duty of signing the temperance pledge. Some societies keep framed and hung upon the wall a temperance pledge with the signatures of all their members. Besides being a fine advertisement for temperance and notification of the temperance principles of the society, this pledge makes a very pleasant souvenir of former members.

Temperance Mass Meetings. In bringing about a temperance reform in your town, emergencies are likely to arise that call for temperance mass meetings, and few agencies can organize these so effectively as the Christian Endeavor societies, especially if they work as a local union. First, as a " drawing card," get some eloquent speaker and advertise him well. You can hardly, however, expect him to treat your local needs. For this purpose open the meeting with a speech, or, better, with four or five short speeches, from well-known local business men and clergymen. It may be that the laws you have are not well enforced. You may greatly need new and more stringent laws. Whatever the theme may be, divide its appropriate sub-topics among the local speakers, and insist on brevity. Of course, if you can get speeches from the present office-holders or from former office-holders, so much the better, provided they are on the right side. Be sure to bring upon the platform — and on the programme, too, if possible — representatives of all political parties.

Decorate the platform brilliantly. Placard the hall with telling temperance mottoes in large type. Get out the band and have it parade around town before the meeting. Form a large temperance chorus from the Christian Endeavorers. Distribute among the audience slips of paper bearing the words of temperance songs, which are to be sung to well-known tunes.

Get the speakers to make as many points as possible by diagrams, and prepare these diagrams for them. Such matters as the number of saloons in town, compared with the number of schools and churches, may be shown by a map. Diagrams may be prepared showing graphically the relative number of arrests in towns with and without saloons. The ratio of drunkards to population, the amount of money received from licenses compared with that paid out for courts, jails, poor-houses, and the like — such telling facts as these may be presented clearly to the eye ; and what gets to the mind that way usually sticks.

Applaud the speakers well. Put all the enthusiasm you can into the meeting. Bring it to a head by the adoption of a ringing resolution. And then go out and *work*, with the understanding that the meeting was only a beginning of the undertaking, after all.

CHAPTER VII.

CHRISTIAN CITIZENSHIP ON HOLIDAYS.

The Use of Holidays. It has become customary in some of the States to use patriotic holidays, such as Washington's Birthday, the Fourth of July, Labor Day, and Patriots' Day, as meeting times for district, county, and city, Christian Endeavor unions. It speaks well for the devotion of our young people that they are willing to sacrifice their holidays to these religious conventions. As might have been expected, the addresses on these days have been tinged with the character of the holiday, so that Christian citizenship has often come to the front, and many a local-union programme has been made up entirely along Christian-citizenship lines. By the use of such holidays, Christian-citizenship committees will get an opportunity for the implanting of much good seed.

On Memorial Day. If your town has a Grand Army post, or any association of old soldiers, you will simply offer your services to them and put yourselves under their direction for the celebration of Memorial Day. They will be glad of your aid in decorating, in singing, in obtaining the flowers. If the young people have any organization that can fitly parade, the veterans would be glad to be joined by it.

But if the old soldiers are not numerous enough to take the day into their own hands, — and before long, alas ! the old soldiers will have passed away, — then very appropriately the Christian Endeavor societies may take up the task of providing some proper memorial services, and of decorating the graves of our honored dead.

A speaker should be obtained for an address, and the best speaker you can find. Have the old soldiers sit on the platform, if even one is in your midst. To fill out and vary the exercises, in addition to the address you .may make use of some of the following Christian Endeavor contributions : —

A flag salute.

A patriotic anthem and other patriotic songs.

Appropriate Scripture verses, or a long passage from the Bible repeated in concert.

War poems, recited by the Endeavorers and the Juniors.

Striking anecdotes of war times, showing the bravery and devotion of the soldiers.

Tributes to the great men of the war ; brief extracts.

" Our town in the war " — a paper of reminiscences gathered from talks with the old people.

Sentence prayers for the nation.

Open meeting, with testimony from all that will : " What my country has a right to expect of me."

Washington's and Lincoln's Birthdays. More suitable occasions there could not be for the emphasizing of patriotic lessons than the birthdays of these great patriots. If nothing else is done, the Christian-citizenship committee should see that the Christian Endeavor prayer meeting nearest to the birthday contains something appropriate to the day. It will be fine, however, if you can get the society to hold on the exact anniversary a special birthday meeting. You will place in some conspicuous position portraits of the hero to be treated. You will decorate the room with national emblems. You will obtain patriotic music. You will get some eloquent speaker for the chief attraction, and yet in some way you will work the Endeavorers themselves into the programme, using a few of the following briefly indicated plans.

For Washington's Birthday : Short essays of not more than five minutes each on " Washington's Christianity," " Washington's Mother," " Washington's Wife," " Washington's Bravery," " Washington's Personal Habits," " Washington's Home," " Washington as a General," " Washington as President." Extracts from Washington's writings. Brief anecdotes about Washington. Open parliament: " What I most admire in George Washington." Symposium : " Lessons our country needs to learn from Washington." Poems about Washington.

For Lincoln's Birthday : Five-minute essays : " Lincoln's Religious Belief," " Lincoln's Boyhood," " Lincoln's Modesty," " Lincoln's Courage," " Lincoln as an Orator," " Lincoln as a Lawyer," " Lincoln as President," " Lincoln's Death," " Lincoln as a Writer." Some of Lincoln's anecdotes. Some anecdotes about Lincoln, showing his kindness of

heart, his keen good sense, his trust in God, his ha-
tred of shams, etc. Tributes to Lincoln from great
writers. Open parliament: "What I should like to
imitate in Lincoln's character." Symposium: "What
Lincoln did for this country." Quotations from Lincoln's speeches and writings.

You may be fortunate enough to get a talk from
some one that has seen Lincoln; at any rate, from
some one that remembers his times. You will doubtless be able to find and place on exhibition some copy
of a newspaper published at the time of the assassination, or other relic of those days.

Thanksgiving Day. In some towns the good old
custom of a Thanksgiving Day service in the church
is falling into disuse. If this is the case in your town,
petition for its revival, on patriotic grounds if on no
higher. If there are clergymen to take it in charge,
the Endeavorers will probably have little to do except
to decorate the church and possibly provide the
music. But they can help greatly by advertising the
meeting and by getting out their friends. It may
happen, however, that the Endeavorers themselves
must take charge of the meeting, if there is one; and,
at any rate, the Christian Endeavor prayer meeting
next to Thanksgiving Day always has a Thanksgiving
topic, and the patriotic work of the Christian-citizenship committee may find in some of these ways an
abundant field. At their own meeting, then, or at
others where they must take a more or less conspicuous part, the Endeavorers may introduce portions of
the following exercises: —

Recitation of some appropriate poem, such as Whittier's " For an Autumn Festival " or Alice Cary's " Thanksgiving."

Concert repetition of some appropriate Psalm, such as the one hundredth or the twenty-third.

Repetition of Thanksgiving and patriotic Bible verses by the members.

Sentence prayers of Thanksgiving, especially remembering our national blessings. Follow this by a series of sentence prayers of petition for the coming year, especially remembering our country's dangers and needs.

A series of two-minute papers or talks : " Some of the blessings our country has received from God this past year "; " Reasons why we are grateful for our nation "; " Under what conditions will God continue his favor to our land? "

A patriotic song by the Juniors.

Brief descriptions, by different Endeavorers, of conditions in lands less fortunate than ours.

Opening of a thanksgiving-box, to which each Endeavorer has contributed some brief expression of thankfulness for some particular blessing. Let a good speaker read these and comment on them.

Close the meeting with the Doxology.

Be sure to receive an offering for the poor, and also ask all to bring gifts of food and clothing.

CHAPTER VIII.

THE RESCUE OF THE FOURTH.

THE good old ways of celebrating the Fourth of July, which made of it a day for the true revival of patriotism, are passing even out of memory in many parts of our country. To restore them to popular favor would be as noble work for better citizenship as any Christian Endeavor society could undertake. If the reader of this page is a citizen of some land other than the United States, it may be that his national holidays also are becoming days for mere merry-making, and that not of the highest type, in which case these suggestions may be adapted to meet his needs.

If your society wishes to reform the celebration of the Fourth in your community, it must begin early, before other and less wise plans have been formed, and anticipate them. Advertise widely your intention. Print full accounts of the preparations. When the programme is ready, have it inserted in the town paper. Use handbills and posters. Set people to talking about it. Make folks think that something is coming.

All the better if you can persuade the societies in some neighboring town to take up the same plans as yours, and co-operate with you. You might thus effect a trade of speakers, the orators from each town going to the other, where they are less known and where people will be more eager to hear them.

Your success will depend largely upon the number of persons you interest in the exercises by giving them an actual part in them. The schools and the Sunday schools and the Christian Endeavor societies, the preachers, the teachers, the lawyers, the editors, the singers and the brass bands, young folks and old folks, — all must be worked in. Be sure not to leave out the Catholics ; they too are Americans. On this day of all days permit no lines of sectarianism to be drawn, or of race. Be especially careful to give adequate representation to all political parties, that it may be recognized as a strictly non-partisan affair.

Appropriate decorations have eloquent part in a sensible Fourth of July. In some public way ask that all stores and houses be decorated at least by the hanging out of one flag. The platform for the speakers should be gorgeous with red, white, and blue, brilliant with the season's flowers, and suggestive with a map of the United States and pictures of the capitol at Washington and some of our great men. Obtain little flag badges for every one, if possible. If you have no liberty pole in your town, what better time than this to raise one, with appropriate ceremonies, triumphantly hauling to the top as fine a flag as the town can afford ?

A procession is another fitting scenic feature, and one of especial value because of the number it interests in your plans for the day. The boys will like to organize in companies bearing banners, American shields, the State seal, and other fitting emblems. Drum corps and brass bands will be available. Symbolic floats are not impossible. At least you may mount Uncle Sam on one cart and Columbia in another, and fill a third with thirteen maidens grouped to represent the original thirteen States and singing patriotic songs. The Grand Army post, the Sons of Veterans, and many another organization will be glad to join the parade, and there will be room also for bicycle clubs and other social groups, to say nothing of the Sunday schools and Christian Endeavor societies, that will after all furnish the backbone of the procession.

Do not think that because you are seeking to reform the observance of the Fourth of July, therefore you must be so dignified as to drive away all the fun. A jolly series of out-of-door contests may be planned and carried out, and the address at the close of them, which will be all the more enjoyed because of them, will point out the connection between strong bodies and the service of our country, and show how a good citizen must keep his body pure and active. Amateur bicycle races and foot races, leaping contests, throwing the hammer, casting the discus, archery, — contests in sports of all kinds which can be witnessed by large companies of people, would aid the celebration greatly. Suitable prizes might be offered to stimulate these — prizes such as a silk flag, a bust of Lincoln, a fine portrait of Washington, a good history of the nation.

It may be best — certainly, if both your physical and literary exercises are brief — to have them all in the afternoon. This arrangement will dispense with any picnic features, and greatly simplify the whole affair, making it possible for many to enjoy the celebration that might not take the trouble to pack up lunch and go off to some distant picnic grounds.

But you must be sure to provide for maintaining the interest indoors in case it rains. For this reason it will be best to obtain the use of a hall for the speech-making.

You will have programmes printed as nicely as you can — possibly in red and blue ink on white paper. Give on this programme a full list of the athletic contests, with the names of all the participants. Get Uncle Sam in traditional costume, or some beautiful girl dressed as Columbia, to preside over these exercises in the hall.

The musical part of the programme should be packed full of interest. Organize as large a chorus as you can. Open with a patriotic song service led by this chorus, the words being placed on the programmes. Introduce one song by the very little tots, and another song by the men alone. The little folks may also be given Scripture verses to be repeated in concert; the older children may give a few brief patriotic recitations. A flag drill, performed on the stage by a group of graceful girls, would please everybody.

By all means have the Declaration of Independence read, and read, too, by the very best reader in the

community. You might add, also, a brief selection
from the writings of Washington or of Lincoln.

Apportion the religious exercises among the clergymen of all faiths. Especially fitting would be a series
of very brief prayers from all the ministers in town,
one following the other.

As to the orator, make no mistake. Appoint no
one merely out of compliment or curiosity. Far better have no oration at all than have one that bores
the people and tires them. If you can't obtain a
speaker of ability, one you can trust to interest and
delight as well as instruct, you will do almost as well
by enlisting in the service a few speakers of less ability. Insisting on brevity, get them to speak in swift
succession on a group of related themes. The variety
you thus obtain will hold people's attention. A most
inspiring series of five-minute talks, for instance,
might be entitled, " A Five-minute Lesson from
Washington," " From Jefferson," " From Samuel
Adams," " From Lincoln," " From Garfield." Instruct each speaker merely to tell a single anecdote
and draw one lesson from it. Another suitable series
of talks would be : " Our county: how big ? How
great ? How loved ? How served ? " Still others
are : " Our country's foes : strong drink ; municipal
misrule ; love of money " ; " Our national foundation
stones : the public school ; the church ; the press ;
our homes." The last series would gain in effective-
ness if each speaker carried out with him a great
pasteboard cube painted to represent stone, and
marked with the theme on which he was to speak.

Close such a meeting with a salute of the flag. The audience is asked to rise, and their attention is called to a placard bearing in plain letters these words : " I pledge allegiance to my flag, and to the country for which it stands — one nation indivisible, with liberty and justice for all." They are asked to raise their right hands, and when a flag is unfurled as a signal, they will repeat those words in concert, thus closing the exercises in a most impressive way.

If you wish to end the day in the orthodox fashion with fireworks, you can greatly improve on the ordinary method by a little co-operation. Simply appoint a committee which will request all house-holders to hand to it the money they would otherwise spend for fireworks, that it may be placed in a common fund. A really magnificent display may thus be bought, and, being set off by experienced hands in a suitable place, it can be seen without danger by all. And thus will close in a burst of glory your model Fourth of July.

CHAPTER IX.

THE CITIZEN REACHING DOWN.

Christian Endeavor in Prison. A most remarkable work is being accomplished by Christian Endeavor in our State prisons and county and city jails, although only a few societies thus far are laboring in this important field. Certainly when we remember what a menace to our nation is its criminal class, we shall decide that no better Christian-citizenship task is possible for us than to seek the reformation of the prisoners. This is a missionary work right at our doors, and the rewards that come from it are many and glorious.

Blessed results have been accomplished by the Christian Endeavor societies among the prisoners in the New York State prison at Albany, in the State prisons of Wisconsin, **Indiana, Kentucky, and Ne-**vada. Chaplains are most earnest in their praise of this instrumentality, and wardens say that their prisons are different places since the advent of Christian Endeavor. Not a few most hopeful conversions have already sprung from this work, conversions that have proved themselves by consecrated lives after release from prison. In some cases already missionary workers and preachers of the gospel have come from prison Christian Endeavor societies.

But the field is as yet scarcely touched, especially the field of the common jails, where the work is different, to be sure, but equally necessary and blessed. Separate societies may undertake the work, but, if a local union exists, much force will be gained by placing the matter under union auspices.

First talk with the chaplain. Explain to him what Christian Endeavor is, if he does n't know. Get his cordial sympathy, permission, and co-operation. You can do little without him. Together with him go to the warden and interest him in the plan.

Then, before you attempt any public meeting, visit with the men as much as possible in private. Get your best workers, the big-hearted, tactful, wise young men and women, to make friends with the prisoners, leave good literature with them, especially bright Christian Endeavor literature, and, if the way opens, to pray with them.

Do not attempt to form a Christian Endeavor society until you have held some meetings with the prisoners. Bring a band of sweet-voiced Endeavorers to the regular religious exercises of the prison, and let them sing their best. Follow this with a short talk, as brisk and cheery and as full of our Christian Endeavor sunshine as you can get it. Keep this up for a few weeks until the prisoners know you for their friends, and look forward with eagerness to your coming.

In the meantime you will have learned who are the more promising among the prisoners, and you will have explained the Christian Endeavor society to them, or refreshed and corrected their previous knowledge of it. It is now time, in conjunction with the chaplain, to form your society. Begin with a very few, if necessary, but with none that do not understand and mean what they are doing. You cannot make your rules too strict. Dismission from the society should immediately follow failure to live up to the pledge. Prison discipline is stern, and Christian discipline must not appear in any way lax.

As for the rest, their meetings will run much as meetings outside the stone walls. Indeed, the more they can be brought in touch with outside Endeavorers, the better for them; and the better, usually, for the outside Endeavorers. Visit their society often. Pray with them, and, in your own societies, pray for them. Remember what a terrible struggle they have entered upon, and how sorely they need all the aid their Christian friends can give them. Write them letters often and get distant Endeavorers to send them letters, to be read to their society, and make them feel less isolated and alone. Especially remember them at the holiday seasons, and make them times of genuine spiritual joy and uplift to them, And, above all, whenever one of these prison Endeavorers goes out into the world again, surround him with all the safeguards that consecrated Christian ingenuity and warm brotherly love can suggest, and do all in your power to keep him firm amid the thousands of temptations and discouragements that will at once beset him.

If by this prison work you succeed in rescuing only a few from the bonds of the evil one, and in making them good citizens and loyal Christians, what a magnificent work for Christian citizenship you will have accomplished!

Ice-Water Tanks. Many men are habitually thirsty, and in warm weather, especially, their thirst becomes a fierce passion. Who is there of us, for that matter, that has not at times, with much exaggeration to be sure, and yet with genuine feeling, exclaimed, "I am half dead with thirst"? Now in most of our cities there is no place where a thirsty man can get a good drink for nothing, and with the exception of the soda-water fountains, whose usefulness in the temperance cause is not recognized as it should be, there is no place save the saloons where he can get a drink for money.

A very practical and effective temperance measure, therefore, and one easily within the possibilities of all our city unions, is the establishing of ice-water tanks on street corners where many men pass. For some time this plan has been carried out by the Cleveland Endeavorers and those in St. Paul, and with well-marked results. Saloons in the neighborhood of these cold-water missionaries have felt their competition.

The cost of the work is easily figured up. It depends, of course, upon the cost of ice and water in your city. The Endeavorers themselves should be willing to do the work connected with the tanks.

Possibly the best plan is this. Take a large wooden cask and place inside it a coil of pipe, which is put in direct connection with the city water supply, so that fresh water enters automatically as the drinkers draw it off.   In the centre of this coil of pipe the ice is placed.   An arrangement with the ice-men can be made so that they will see that the ice supply is kept up.   Paint upon the cask the name of the union, and a hearty invitation to partake.   The different societies will like to divide this work among them, each paying for its own cask, which will bear the name of that particular society.

In Lounging Places.   The spots where men have leisure to read and where they meet in large numbers afford magnificent seed ground for Christian-citizen-ship work.   To furnish good literature, and especially literature bearing on the duties of a citizen, to such places as our railroad stations, is a very obvious duty of those at work for better citizenship.   The barber shops are usually provided with the lightest of flimsy literature, the engine houses of the fire department, the corridors of the hotels, the post-offices where men wait for mail — there are many such places that are open for seed-sowing.   Some Endeavorers have even fixed boxes, protected from the water, on the backs of the seats in the parks, and filled them with good reading matter.   The Endeavorers themselves may easily be induced to furnish from their homes just what is wanted in the way of papers and magazines. Do not permit anything dull to get into these boxes or upon the Christian Endeavor tables.   Every piece of literature must be good, but none goody-goody. Keep the tables well up to date.   Insert now and then some manly tract on the responsibility of a citizen, or on some specific phase of reform. Watch for results, and you will see them.

Potato Farms. Potato farms, or " Pingree patches," as they are named from the governor of Michigan, who originated this form of charity, afford a very sensible mode of relief for the poor, especially in cities. A Christian Endeavor society that wishes to start this plan, will seek out the owners of unoccupied land, land held for building, and will get as many of them as possible to permit this land to be planted in vegetables such as potatoes. It will next be necessary to obtain a fund for the purchase of tools and seeds. You may persuade some benevolent farmers to do the ploughing for nothing. Finally, make wide advertisement of the plan, and induce the poor to try it, each taking a portion of the ground and cultivating it for his own use. You will need to obtain the services of some one wise in practical agriculture, to direct these amateur farmers.

The plan, it will be seen, cannot be carried out without much work, but it is well worth carrying out, because it is teaching the poor to help themselves, and that is the best of all charities. In many towns and cities this method has been tried, and it has met with uniform success. It has preserved the self-respect of thousands of men, and has kept thousands of families from starvation or from becoming public charges. Full information concerning this important work may be obtained from the New York Society for Improving the Condition of the Poor.

CHAPTER X.

FOR SABBATH OBSERVANCE.

OF course the first and best way to promote a better observance of the Lord's day is for the Endeavorers to keep it holy themselves, and the Christian-citizenship committee must begin at home. At some meeting especially devoted to the subject the matter should be set before the society with frankness and firmness. Talk about Sunday studying for Monday's lessons, about the Sunday newspapers and the reading of other secular literature on the Lord's day, about Sunday letter-writing, Sunday bicycle-riding and carriage-riding and boating.

But you will waste your time if you merely indulge in these negatives and do not go on to show what kind of reading makes a blessed Sabbath, what kind of exercise is permissible upon the Lord's day, how far the day may be made one of social enjoyment, and what occupations will fill it with the true spirit of rest and recreation. Especially, make a plea for more and better family life on Sunday. Our strenuous living, each bent as for life upon his own task, keeps us far apart on week-days, but Sunday should be the day of reunion.

You might hold a symposium on the subject, " The

happiest Sunday I ever spent." A Sunday question-box would make another valuable feature of such a meeting. Ask the Endeavorers to come with questions written out bearing upon Sabbath observance, — any difficulties they may wish solved for themselves or others. Put your wisest and readiest man in charge of this question-box. Let the evening somewhere contain an account — from books or from the lips of some traveller — of Sunday as it is observed — or, rather, *not* observed — on the continent of Europe. Show the Endeavorers some of the evils that have already come upon those nations from this failure to keep God's law of rest and worship. At the close of the evening, the society members may be asked to give some expression of their decisions in the matter. This may take the form of a resolution and a vote, of a pledge by uplifted hands, or of signatures to a formal printed pledge, — whichever your pastor may think wise.

Then, outside the society much work may be done for the purification of the Sabbath. The post-offices may be kept open on that day, — an entirely needless profanation of its holy hours. A petition signed by a majority of the town's people and sent to the postmaster general at Washington, would probably result in the closing of the office on Sunday ; I say " probably," because, in the absence of law on the subject, so much depends on the temper of the authorities. A concerted action among the patrons of barber shops and meat markets might result in their closing their doors on the Lord's day. An arrangement might be made whereby the drugstores of the place should alternate in keeping open on Sunday. If Sunday papers are largely taken, much good might be done by introducing newspapers — if good ones are accessible — that do not print Sunday editions, and persuading the church-members, at least, to subscribe for them. About obtaining the enforcement of laws regarding the Sabbath, I have spoken elsewhere.

Enforcing Temperance and Sunday Laws. What is said under this head will apply as well, of course, to the enforcement of any law pertaining to the morals of the community. I can speak only in general terms, so much depends on the form of government under which you live; whether, for instance, you are in a large city or a small village. In any event, if the laws are not enforced, and the older Christians will not take the matter up, there is every reason why the younger Christians should do what they can to improve the disgraceful state of affairs.

First, move on the men whose business it is to enforce the law. It leads only to mischief when, with whatever good intentions, a body of citizens set themselves to do the work that should be done by officers elected for that purpose. Go first to the lowest officer whose duty it is to move in the matter. It may be a policeman or the town marshal or the constable. Point out the law and respectfully ask him to enforce it. If no results follow, pass to the next highest officer. In a small Western city — many of these cities contain only two or three thousand persons — this will be the mayor. In a large city it will be some police sergeant or the chief of police. Set before him the facts and state what you have already done. If need be, keep on, passing to the police commissioner, the mayor, if it is a large city, or the prosecuting attorney of the city or county or even of the State.

Of course this takes for granted that you know the law thoroughly, and that you are advised by good lawyers at every step. Never go alone to any of these officers, — at least for a final visit, — but get their decisive word in the presence of as many witnesses as you can draw together. If you can interest in the case some influential citizen, obtain him for your spokesman. Do not seek to appear in the matter at all, but seek rather the success of your cause.

If the officials are obdurate, sneering, and abusive, — as in the case of a long-standing tolerance of iniquity may well be the fact, — seek publicity for your plea. Go into the papers with vigorous articles. Get the laws in question printed on broadsides, and post them up everywhere with introductory appeals. Get the ministers to preach on the subject. Hold an indignation meeting and pass condemnatory resolutions. Obtain signatures to a paper emphatically calling upon the authorities for the enforcement of the law.

If the authorities, as likely, plead ignorance of the violation of the law and call for evidence, get it in abundance. You may need to hire detectives, but probably not. Combine with a large number in gathering this evidence, so that your opponents may see that persecution is futile. You may need to be sworn in as special police. Never attempt arrests; that is not your business. Never carry revolvers; they will get you into more trouble than they save you from. Make your evidence as circumstantial as possible. Let a lawyer pass upon it before you rely on it. When you have obtained it all, present it to the proper authorities. If they do not heed it, put it into print, and present it to the people back of the authorities, and you will get a hearing.

The trouble may be that there is no ordinance covering the ground, or that the ground is inadequately covered by the laws already passed. If so, agitate for better laws. Get the best men available to draw up the law for you. Hold a mass meeting to discuss it and win friends for it. Print it in the papers. Get signatures to a petition embodying it. Having thus made all the friends for the ordinance you can, inform the council that you wish, at some convenient meeting, to present a petition in person, and request them to set a time for a hearing, which they will hardly refuse. Get as many strong men as you can to go with you to this hearing. Obtain some forcible speakers to urge the claims of the law upon your city lawmakers. Much will depend upon the array of influence you can thus focus upon the petition. When action is taken upon the matter, note with care who votes against it, and enter into an active campaign against them, if they are renominated. Do not be discouraged if your first efforts meet with absolute failure. You will have done much if you do nothing but arouse public sentiment. Never give up till you conquer.

And then — a most necessary caution — after victory, *ceaseless vigilance*, which alone, in all matters of moral reform, is the price of continued victory.

CHAPTER XI.

SOME CHRISTIAN-CITIZENSHIP CRUSADES.

Humane Work. Where men and women, boys and girls, are cruel to the brutes, they are almost certain to be cruel to one another, coarse in their feelings, and brutal in their conduct. Whatever can be done, with the young especially, to make them more gentle toward these helpless wards of man will hasten the day when lynch law will disappear, and prize fights be forgotten, and war itself be no more.

If you will write to the American Society for the Prevention of Cruelty to Animals (New York), they will send you full instructions for the formation of Bands of Mercy among the young. These organizations may be made helpful adjuncts to the Junior society. In most cases, it will probably be better to avoid multiplying organizations, and simply form a " humane committee " or a " Band of Mercy committee," whose work it will be to hold occasional meetings in the interests of the dumb animals, and to present often, at the regular meeting, interesting items concerning animals and how they should be treated.

Among their elders also there is room for work.

Who with any kindness of heart has not longed to be clothed with police power when seeing a horse cruelly beaten because it could not pull a load much too heavy for it ? or when seeing some dog or cat abandoned to starvation ? In every community there should be laws requiring proper treatment of domestic animals, and these laws the Endeavorers can get passed. An occasional letter to the papers describing some particular case of neglect will do good. The town government may be persuaded to give the powers of deputy or special policeman for this purpose to men of character and intelligence that desire to put a stop by immediate action — which alone, in many cases, is of any use — to the shocking brutality of some drivers and owners of animals.

Anti-cigarette Leagues. The establishment of anti-cigarette leagues among the boys of our public schools, starting, I believe, in New York City, has now spread so widely that nearly all large cities have tried the beneficent plan. There is a simple pledge of abstinence from cigarette-smoking, a button or other badge of membership, and an occasional meeting to discuss the evils of cigarette-smoking and to arouse interest on the part of those that are not yet members. The boys themselves, once the league is started, make vigorous canvassers for it. They delight in "belonging," and soon come to consider it more manly to refrain from smoking than before they thought it to smoke. Cigarette-smoking is becoming so serious an evil and threatens to work so great mischief among our future citizens, that the establishment of such leagues as this among the school-boys is magnificent work for Christian citizenship. It must be done with the aid of the school superintendent and teachers, and the young men of the societies are the ones to present the matter to the boys, and to join the league with them.

Good Roads. I urge all Christian-citizenship committees to take an interest in the question of better roads. Notwithstanding all that has been written and said of late years on this important subject, there yet remains much popular ignorance of the value of good roads, and the injury to the community, not only as regards their worldly prosperity but as to their higher interests, from roads that are poorly constructed and lazily maintained. Where the roads are long sloughs, the isolation of the people leads to stagnation. All kinds of religious interests suffer. Social gatherings are made difficult. The people cannot get to church, nor the children to school. The cost of marketing being increased, they have less money for good purposes. And all this without mention of the great gain that comes from the very sight of neat highways thriftily kept up.

It will be worth while for the Christian-citizenship committee to study the right ways of making roads, and successful plans for paying for their construction and maintenance. A lecture on road-making may be obtained, illustrated with magic-lantern pictures of good roads, bad roads, and processes of construction. All the town may be invited in to listen. The young folks and their ideas will be laughed at by many, but if you can procure the building of a single sample bit of road according to the proper fashion, the sneers will soon change to approval, and farmers and merchants and bicycle-riders and pedestrians, pleasure drivers and those that propel baby carriages, will unite to call you blessed!

Indecent Posters. In many cities most disgraceful posters are permitted upon the bill-boards, especially those that advertise theatrical performances. If there is a law against such things, the Christian Endeavorers can see that it is enforced. Experience has shown how it may be done. Appeal to the chief of police. That failing, appeal to the district attorney or the mayor. Write to the papers. Urge the ministers to preach sermons directed against the evil. You will not go far in this course before the objectionable posters will come down.

Of course, if you have no law to which you can appeal, you must first agitate for one, using the methods for that purpose elsewhere described. The evil of these posters is so positive, so glaring, so insidious and deadly, that to eradicate it is well worth a long fight and much self-sacrifice.

No Sunday Bicycling. The use of the bicycle on the Lord's day for purposes of mere pleasure has seriously threatened the Sabbath, and the preservation of a day of rest and worship is so important for public welfare that any Christian-citizenship committee is thoroughly justified in becoming also a committee to regulate the use of the bicycle on Sunday. One of the best ways to agitate the matter, and at the same time crystallize results, is the formation of a No-Sun-day-Bicycle League. The members of this league sign a pledge promising not to use their wheels on the Lord's day for mere recreation. The pledge might read : '' Believing that God's law, written not only in his Book but in the constitution of our bodies and the needs of society, requires the observance of one day in seven as a day of rest and worship, I hereby promise to make no use of my bicycle on Sunday, except in case of necessity or when about the King's business." Members of this league might wear some distinctive ribbon upon their wheels, bearing some such motto as " Member of the No-Sunday-Bicycle League. One day in seven for rest and worship."

CHAPTER XII.

A BUDGET OF PLANS AND SUGGESTIONS.

Work with the Pastors. There is no danger in suggesting to young people this work for better citizenship, if they will seek the guidance of older heads; but unless they do this, there is danger that the Christian Endeavor union and the cause of the movement at large may be brought into disrepute by the zeal, not according to knowledge, of some hot-head who may wish the union to indorse some particular candidate or political party, or embark the Endeavorers in some visionary scheme, all with the best purposes in the world. No step along the lines laid out in this book should be taken without the full co-operation and consent of the pastors of the churches involved. They are the natural and proper guides of the Christian Endeavor societies in all their undertakings, and wherever there is the slightest possibility of a misunderstanding, they should be consulted.

For this and similar objects every Christian Endeavor union should organize a pastors' advisory board — a body of pastors fairly representing all denominations, to whom the union officers can go whenever they are, or should be, in doubt. This advisory board may be made up by appointment from the various denominational ministers' meetings of the city, or, if the town is a small one, it may consist of all the ministers in the place. To avoid confusion, its members should serve for long periods or for life. If the pastors are given an earnest invitation to form such a board and are not willing, they will have no right to criticise the Christian Endeavor union for acts which their wiser counsel would have prevented. This plan has been tried in some unions already. The pastors enter into it with heartiness, and the results are altogether good.

Calling for Sermons. It has become quite a fashion for reform organizations to call upon the pastors, or urge the Endeavorers to call upon the pastors, for sermons on a certain Sunday upon some needed reform. I sometimes suspect that if pastors should heed all such appeals they would have no opportunity at all to preach upon their own topics. Our Endeavorers should so seldom make requests of this kind that they will mean something when they come. And never make them without some guarantee of attendance and a decided effort to get others to come. Do not fix a time for the sermon, but present to your pastor a cordially worded invitation to preach the sermon, signed by all the members of the society, and let this invitation ask that the society may be notified of the day when the sermon will be preached, because they wish not only to be sure to be there themselves, but to invite all their friends. That will be an invitation the pastor will be glad to get.

Patriotic Songs. Our nation is not rich in patriotic songs. All the more disgraceful is it that so few of us should know well the few songs we have. Start "The Star-Spangled Banner" in any company, and note how many voices fall off after the first stanza. It is quite as bad with other national songs, and even "America" we are not all sure of. The Christian-citizenship committee will do well to make a collection of patriotic hymns and songs, copying them on some duplicator, and drilling the society in them on all proper occasions till every Endeavorer knows them and can sing them with his eyes shut.

The Use of Flags. Every citizen should own a good, large, American flag ; but alas ! there are many American homes, I fear, that could not muster even a little one. It is an excellent custom not only to decorate our houses with national emblems on the great patriotic holidays, but also to keep the flag on view in some living room all the time. This custom the Christian Endeavor society may recommend to others and adopt themselves. By getting the flags in quantity, they may obtain them much more cheaply.

I have spoken elsewhere about the custom of raising the flag over the school-house. It should fly also over all public buildings, especially over the post-office, the city hall, the building where your town council meets, — every building of the kind. If your community has not yet awaked to the importance of this silent display of patriotism, let your society raise the money and buy a few flags for presentation to the town. The occasion of the presentation and flag-raising may be made fruitful in the interests of better citizenship.

Village Improvement Societies. In many a small town a village improvement society would put new life into the place, and the zeal for the public good aroused by its undertakings would go on to larger matters. There is no reason why Endeavorers should not lead in the formation of such a society. The steps are simple. First talk the matter over quietly with a few leading citizens and make sure of their co-operation. Get together a small company of men — it would be a question to be decided in each community for itself whether women should be admitted — and fix upon the next step in consultation with them. Probably you will next issue a general call, stating the object of the proposed society, and asking all that would like to join to meet at a certain place and time, to form a constitution and elect officers. This call could be sent out through the papers or by posters. You should have a simple constitution ready to submit, in order to save time.

What a village improvement society may do depends of course on the condition of the village. The streets may need bettering. Tree-planting may be in order. You may have no names on the street corners. The town bulletin boards may well be replaced by larger and neater ones. Rubbish in the streets and in the back-yards may disfigure the town. A campaign for the removal of fences may add to the town's attractiveness. The character of the town paper may be improved. The surroundings of the railroad station, by which so many form their opinion of the place, may be very disagreeable.

You may take up larger matters, such as the possible building of an electric street railway, better street lighting, better protection from fire, the introduction of water works and gas, the drawing to the town of new manufacturing enterprises.

Nor will a village improvement society hold its hands from the moral problems of the town. For the safety of the children, it may press upon the town council the adoption of a curfew law. It may decide that the town has too many saloons, and initiate a temperance crusade. If any company of earnest men consider for some time the improvement of their community, they can hardly fail to see that the greatest possible improvement is an improvement in the character of its inhabitants. In many ways, then, our Christian Endeavor societies would be doing true work for Christian citizenship, if they should set themselves to the founding of village improvement societies.

Debates and Lyceums. The day of the old-fashioned lyceum has gone by; but Christian Endeavor can bring it back again, and it would be a genuine service to the world to do so. The public debating of public questions and discussion more or less formal of public events — the principle of the New England town meeting — is something we dare not relegate to our newspapers. We young people should train ourselves to public debate. There is much in the clash of speech and the friction of opposing antagonists for the loss of which type can never compensate.

A splendid thing for a Christian-citizenship committee to do, therefore, is to organize a current-topic class; or, if you wish, let it be a regular lyceum of the old, stalwart type. Get a leader, if you can, — some man well versed in history, especially in modern history; a man that can fill out for you the brief foreign items in the papers, tell you more about men and movements, and interpret to you what is going on in the world. Every meeting might open with a talk by your leader, followed, of course, by a brisk questioning, first by the class and then by him.

But if you have no such capable leader, nevertheless you can carry on a current-topic class most effectively. Gather together as many earnest, wide-awake young people as you can — young women as well as young men, for the young women read the newspapers nowadays, and why should they not? Divide up the world among yourselves. If there are only five of you, give each a grand division. You may have enough to take a nation apiece, China to one, France to another, Madagascar to a third. What you have thus done for the world at large, repeat for your own country, giving each a section — the East, the central States, the mountain States, etc., if you are few; giving each a single State, if you are sufficiently numerous.

This division having been made, each member is expected as soon as possible to make himself an authority in his field, both home and abroad. Whatever of interest happens there, he will report. Any questions the club may ask him about his field, he will be expected to answer. He will be called upon occasionally for a talk on recent events in his field, and always, whenever the eyes of the world are turned upon it, the eyes of the club will be turned upon him.

If at any time the interest in any direction becomes intense enough to warrant it, several may be transferred to that field. In the case of our war with Spain, for instance, the entire club might be set to study it and report on it, one taking in charge the matter of volunteers, another the militia, a third Spain, a fourth the other nations of Europe with reference to the war, a fifth our navy, a sixth the Philippines, etc.

Some part of each meeting should be set apart for words from each reporter, whether anything of especial interest is going on in his country or not. Occasionally, longer papers and talks should be required from all the members. For the sake of thoroughness, each should be kept in one field till he has become somewhat familiar with it; but, for the sake of gaining wide views, there should be a regular system of transference from one country to another. A current-topic class such as this, with frequent debates and discussions, cannot fail to be of the very greatest interest, and to train its members at the same time for better citizenship.

The Post-office Referendum. Some day our people will put themselves in as close touch with their legislators as the people of Switzerland, who, by the processes of the initiative and the referendum, can

themselves propose laws or require their reference to
themselves. Till that day comes, the free use of
Uncle Sam's mails is the next best mode of influencing legislation, and of letting our representatives
know what sort of opinions they are to represent.
The Christian-citizenship committee will do a grand
thing, if it teaches the Endeavorers, especially the
voters among them, to write to their State and national representatives whenever they have any special
desire for certain action on their part.

To this end the committee should have a list of
names and addresses of all these statesmen, and
should learn just the proper form of address for each,
— which is simply : " To the Honorable John Smith,
Massachusetts House of Representatives, Boston," or,
" Ohio State Senate, Columbus, Ohio," or, " House
of Representatives, Washington," or, " United States
Senate, Washington."

One very important point to note in this patriotic
work is this, that not all the letters should be fault-
finding. When you approve of the stand taken by
your representative, when he has made an eloquent
speech whose sentiments you indorse, when he has
cast a brave vote for the right under trying circumstances, why not write and thank him for it ? Such
words of praise will be more effective in influencing
good legislation than words of blame when we think
the course taken has been a wrong one, though such
words, too, should sometimes be spoken.

One other caution : whenever you urge the writing
to legislators, urge the most careful attention to the

composition, the penmanship (better get everything typewritten), the spelling, and all such matters. The post-office referendum will speedily fall into discredit and lose all its power for good, if it is used more by ignorant or careless persons than by the cultivated and thoughtful. I suspect that there is an opinion among legislators that it is chiefly the " cranks " that write to them. We shall be doing a grand work if we change completely the character of their correspondence.

And a final point : remember that your representatives are very busy men, and do not expect a reply. Expressly say in each letter that you do not expect a reply, but that your letter is merely to let him know how one of his constituents feels on the subject. Be brief, pointed, courteous, and intelligent, and your communications will be received with respect and will not fail of result.

Our Workers' Library

Helpful Books for Christian Workers

Only 35 cents each, postpaid.

The Officer's Handbook. By AMOS R. WELLS. 143 pages devoted to the work of the various officers of young people's societies. Special chapters devoted to parliamentary law, reception of new members, etc.

The Missionary Manual. By AMOS R. WELLS. The most complete hand-book of methods for missionary work in young people's societies ever published. 134 pages.

Fuel for Missionary Fires. By BELLE M. BRAIN. 115 pages of practical plans for missionary committees. Everything tried and proved.

Prayer-Meeting Methods. By AMOS R. WELLS. This book contains by far the most comprehensive collection of prayer-meeting plans ever made.

Social Evenings. By AMOS R. WELLS. This is the most widely used collection of games and social entertainments ever made.

Social to Save. By AMOS R. WELLS. A companion volume to "Social Evenings." A mine of enjoyment for the society and home circle.

Our Unions. By AMOS R. WELLS. Wholly devoted to Christian Endeavor unions of all kinds, their officers, work, and conventions.

Weapons for Temperance Warfare. By BELLE M. BRAIN. Full of ammunition for temperance meetings. Hundreds of facts, illustrations, suggestions, programmes.

Next Steps. By REV. W. F. McCAULEY. A book for every Christian Endeavor worker. It is a storehouse of suggestions.

Citizens in Training. By AMOS R. WELLS. A complete manual of Christian citizenship, written especially for those that desire to make their country better.

Eighty Pleasant Evenings. A book of social entertainments, intended for young people's societies, church workers, temperance unions, and for individual use.

UNITED SOCIETY OF CHRISTIAN ENDEAVOR
Boston and Chicago

The Temple Series

This is the handsomest series of holiday books at a low price ever issued. The books are by the best modern authors They are beautifully bound in cloth of dainty shades, stamped with an original cover design in colors and gold. Each volume contains an appropriate half-tone frontispiece.

The Four G's..........................By THEODORE L. CUYLER.
      Grace, Grit, Gratitude and Growth.

Golden Counsels..........................By DWIGHT L. MOODY.
      Practical subjects forcefully presented.

Well-built..................By Rev. THEODORE L. CUYLER, D.D.
      Plain talks to young people.

Helps Upward....................By Rev. WAYLAND HOYT, D.D.
      Apt illustrations of great themes.

A Fence of Trust...........................By MARY F. BUTTS.
      Poems and Sonnets.

Pluck and Purpose...................By WILLIAM M. THAYER.
      Success, and how to attain it.

Little Sermons for One.....................By AMOS R. WELLS.
      Heart to heart talks.

Wise Living.................By Rev. GEORGE C. LORIMER, D.D.
      The gaining and wise use of money.

The Indwelling God......By Rev. CHARLES A. DICKINSON, D.D.
      The power and purpose of a life of faith.

Tact...By KATE SANBORN.
      Racy essays on society's virtues and foibles.

Youth and Age...................By Rev. JAMES STALKER, D.D.
      A suggestive treatment of Ecclesiastes 12.

Sunshine (Poems)...........................By MARY D. BRINE.
      Poems of cheer and encouragement.

Making the Most of Oneself......By Rev. A. S. GUMBART, D.D.
      Practical talks to young men.

Answered! By Rev. J. WILBUR CHAPMAN, D.D., Rev. R. A. TORREY, D.D., Rev. C. H. YATMAN, Rev. EDGAR E. DAVIDSON, THOMAS E. MURPHY, and Rev. A. C. DIXON, D.D.
      Remarkable instances of answered prayer.

Just to Help...............................By AMOS R. WELLS.
      Some poems for every day.

Old Lanterns.........................By Rev. F. E. CLARK, D.D.
      Valuable lessons from Jeremiah.

UNITED SOCIETY OF CHRISTIAN ENDEAVOR
Boston and Chicago

The "How" Series

By AMOS R. WELLS

7 1-4 by 4 1-2 inches in size. Uniformly bound with illuminated cover design. About 150 pages each.
Price, 75 cents.

How to Work

This is a working nation, and yet few among its millions of workers know how to work to the best advantage and with the best results. The fundamental principles of wise labor are set forth in these chapters in a familiar, conversational style. Much of the book consists of actual talks given to young men and women starting out in life. "Puttering," "Putting Off," "Hurry Up!" "Taking Hints," "A Pride in Your Work," "'Can' Conquers," "The Bulldog Grip," "The Trivial Round,"—these are specimen titles of the thirty-one chapters. The book is not didactic, but presents truth in illustrations, so that it *sticks*.

How to Play

The author of this book evidently believes in recreation. The very first chapter is entitled, "The Duty of Playing." Separate chapters are devoted to the principal indoor amusements, conversation and reading being the author's preferences, and also to the leading outdoor sports, especially the bicycle and lawn tennis. There are many practical chapters on such themes as how to kee games fresh, inventing names, what true recreation is, and how to use it to the best advantage. "Flabby Playing," "Playing by Proxy," "Fun that Fits," "Overdoing It,"—these are some of the chapter titles. In one section of the book scores of indoor games are described concisely, but with sufficient fulness.

How to Study

These chapters, on a very practical theme, deal with the most practical aspects of it,—such topics as concentration of mind, night study, cramming, memory-training, care of the body, note-taking, and examinations. The author makes full use of his experience as a teacher in the public schools and as a college professor, and the book is largely made up of talks actually given to his students, and found useful in their work. The chapters are enlivened by many illustrations and anecdotes, and the whole is put into very attractive covers.

UNITED SOCIETY OF CHRISTIAN ENDEAVOR
Boston and Chicago

Recent Religious Books

The Secret of a Happy Day
By Rev. J. WILBUR CHAPMAN, D.D.

6 3-4 x 4 1-2 inches ; 103 pages ; bound in cloth. An excellent half-tone portrait of Dr. Chapman forms the frontispiece.
Price, 50 cents.

The " Daily Quiet Hours " at the Detroit Christian Endeavor Convention were the most remarkable meetings of that great gathering. The addresses given by Dr. Chapman at that time have now been divided into thirty-one chapters, — one for each day of the month — and are included in this volume. The first edition of the book was sold out upon the day of publication. A new edition is now ready. The chapters of the book are based upon the wonderful twenty-third psalm.

The Spiritual Life of the Sunday-School
By Rev. J. WILBUR CHAPMAN, D.D.

6 -3 4 x 4 1 -2 inches, 62 pages ; bound in cloth, 35 cents.

These articles were originally printed in the *Sunday-School Times.* There was such a demand for them that Dr. Chapman has now consented to put them into this permanent form. The book presents very clearly the duties and opportunities of both officers and teachers, and gives some suggestive helps on the preparation necessary for personal work.

The Surrendered Life
By Rev. J. WILBUR CHAPMAN, D.D.

6 3-4 x 4 1 -2 inches ; 70 pages ; bound in cloth ; 50 cents.

This little volume sets forth clearly, simply, and winningly the life " hid with Christ in God," and the way to enter into it. The tasteful binding forms a most fit setting for the contents.

UNITED SOCIETY OF CHRISTIAN ENDEAVOR
Boston and Chicago

www.ingramcontent.com/pod-product-compliance
Lightning Source LLC
Chambersburg PA
CBHW020506030426
42337CB00011B/258